A SOCIOLOGY

The series in Comparative Politics
and International Studies

Series editor, Christophe Jaffrelot

This series consists of translations of noteworthy manuscripts and publications in the social sciences emanating from the foremost French researchers at Sciences Po, Paris. The focus of the series is the transformation of politics and society by transnational and domestic factors—globalisation, migration and the postbipolar balance of power on the one hand, and ethnicity and religion on the other. States are more permeable to external influence than ever before and this phenomenon is accelerating processes of social and political change the world over. In seeking to understand and interpret these transformations, this series gives priority to social trends from below as much as to the interventions of state and non-state actors.

JEAN-LOUIS ROCCA

A Sociology of
Modern China

Translated by

Gregory Elliott
Revised and updated by the author

OXFORD
UNIVERSITY PRESS

OXFORD
UNIVERSITY PRESS

Oxford University Press is a department of the
University of Oxford. It furthers the University's objective
of excellence in research, scholarship, and education
by publishing worldwide.

Oxford   New York

Auckland   Cape Town   Dar es Salaam   Hong Kong   Karachi
Kuala Lumpur   Madrid   Melbourne   Mexico City   Nairobi
New Delhi   Shanghai   Taipei   Toronto

With offices in

Argentina   Austria   Brazil   Chile   Czech Republic   France   Greece
Guatemala   Hungary   Italy   Japan   Poland   Portugal   Singapore
South Korea   Switzerland   Thailand   Turkey   Ukraine   Vietnam

Oxford is a registered trade mark of Oxford University Press
in the UK and certain other countries.

Published in the United States of America by
Oxford University Press
198 Madison Avenue, New York, NY 10016

Rocca, Jean-Louis
A Sociology of Modern China
ISBN 978-0-19-023112-5 hardcover
978-0-19-023120-0 paperback

Printed in India on acid-free paper

To Roxane

CONTENTS

vii

CONTENTS

CONTENTS

INTRODUCTION

More than any other country, China poses a problem to those
seeking to understand it. They seem to be paralysed by the
(supposed) longevity and stability of its civilisation, the size of
its territory and population, its influence, the sudden jolts in its
history, the complexity of its social structures and imaginaries.
People are never neutral on the subject of China. Fascination
is mixed with disapproval, even detestation. There is nothing
new about this. From the sinophilia of the Jesuits, via the anti-
yellow racism of the colonial era, to the Maophilia of the
European intellectual elites in the 1970s, the Middle Kingdom
has always been regarded as a world apart. Today, to over-
come this confusion, and arrive at some certainty, most observers are inclined to prioritise two intellectual frameworks that
are similarly schematic. The first one involves lapsing into cultural essentialism. The Middle Kingdom has allegedly generated a unique, specific world-view that has impregnated the
whole society, and which the Chinese, whatever their personal
background and trajectory, cannot rid themselves of.[1] In sum,
the Chinese 'are not like us'.

In contrast, the second framework insists on the universality
of historical trajectories. Societies supposedly conform to evo-
lutionary rules that China cannot escape. Economic development causes them to converge, from one stage to the next, on
a common model—modernity—that combines the dominance

1

of markets, electoral democracy and the triumph of individuality.[2] Here, China's specificity is not perceived as natural, but the price paid for the variety of social forms and accidents of history in the framework of a universal model. Chinese society is thus characterised by its incompleteness with respect to the model. Its economy is not yet an authentically market one; its state is not completely modern; and the Chinese are not fully-fledged individuals. Such incompleteness is generally regarded as temporary: China will not be able to elude the course of history for long. What must therefore be discovered and understood are the mechanisms of transition that will steer it into harbour. The blockages rendering evolution difficult or chaotic have to be identified. 'The Chinese are like us; it's just that they are taking longer to reach the universal condition.' Consequently, a new discipline has emerged in China studies, 'transitionalism', which aims at studying the progressive changeover from a socialist society to a modern society.[3] Chinese researchers have themselves adopted this practice and have invented a word (*zhuanxing*) for describing it.[4]

The picture is further complicated by the widespread tendency to mix the two frameworks. It is not unusual to find culturalist and modernising references in the same author or speaker, with one prevailing—albeit never definitively—over the other, depending on circumstances. Thus, while many stress the importance of family and kinship bonds in economic or political relations, everyone is trying to discover how the emergence of different rational and legal norms challenges this very Chinese peculiarity. In China itself, it is not uncommon to hear an intellectual say that 'in China, things are different, you need to be Chinese to understand'; or that 'even the Westerners who know China best can't understand some things'; and then, a few minutes later, that 'modernisation is indispensable' and 'China is in transition to modernity'.

Orthodox Thinking

The continual alternation between these two approaches is nothing new and has already given rise to numerous imaginaries in the past. In truth, it betrays a lack of interest in China: it is first and foremost a pretext for talking about other things. The Jesuits' sinophilia was based both on a high estimation of Chinese culture and an evolutionistic standpoint that regarded the enlightened despotism of the emperors as a prefiguration of good government. By contrast, the semi-colonial era of 1840–1949 summoned up an imaginary of China's cultural inferiority and 'backwardness'—shortcomings that could only be corrected by the civilising action of the West. To convince themselves of the necessity of dominating China, 'the developed' nations had to make the inferiority of Chinese society visible and unquestionable to everyone. Finally, Western Maoism combined Chinese 'otherness' ('they offer us a different view of the world') with the projection of a new political horizon (a different society) that was no longer to be found in 'the West' because of the bankruptcy of Soviet Marxism–Leninism. From this standpoint, China represented a new frontier in the intellectual battle against capitalism.

Culturalist Impasses

The main criticism to be made of the culturalist approach is that it reduces our ability to understand. Its clarity, and the 'common sense' it embodies, provide a simple, universal intellectual framework. This explains its widespread diffusion. In bar-room philosophising, as in philosophical or academic circles, it seems to have an answer for everything. Yet as soon as an attempt is made to define the Chinese culture that explains everything, the house of cards collapses. Everyone, be they Chinese or not, has his own conception of Chinese culture.

What 'culture' is being referred to? That of Confucius, the Empire, the Republic, or today? Which region is at issue? A remote town in Sichuan or Shanghai, the great metropolis? Finally, which social type is supposed to be taken as the cultural norm? The major intellectual, the shrewd businessman, the shopkeeper, the member of the urban lower classes, the peasant? The wealthy, the poor, the middling? The hip artist? It suffices to hear a Chinese academic talking about the ordinary Chinese, at best an unskilled worker, at worst a countryman, to realise that we are dealing with at least two different cultures and that Chinese culture is itself … culturalist. According to the elite, this ordinary Chinese is uneducated, impolite, submissive, irrational.

A further difficulty is that an individual's behaviour and cultural discourse will vary with the circumstances and background of his or her interlocutor. A native researcher might criticise the lack of political reform before an audience of compatriots and justify it in discussion with a Westerner. Another one will do the opposite. More prosaically, a 'globalised' Chinese person will make a point of 'doing it the Western way' in a French restaurant, but will immediately forget his worthy resolutions when surrounded by his peers. In short, cultural identity is not a given. It is a set of practices that are certainly rooted in the personality, but which vary enormously depending on context, place and time, which are constantly diversifying and leave enormous room for manipulation, whether conscious or unconscious, of social codes and imaginaries.[5] As for the spectacle of everyday life, it is no more informative about Chinese norms of behaviour. According to contexts, the ordinary Chinese will act differently. The student respects the professor in the classroom, but does not observe the highway code when driving.

The Impasses of Transitionalism

As for modernisation theory, it is inoperative on three counts. Firstly, because the quasi-metaphysical power that is supposed to preside over the destiny of the world exists nowhere on earth.[6] The history of the developed and developing countries has shown that every trajectory is different[7] and that the 'great divide' between tradition and modernity is a flight of fancy.[8] Despite thirty years of exceptional growth and dramatic 'modernisation', not only is China not genuinely democratic—are India or Russia?—but it is hard to determine whether the Chinese are already modern or still 'traditional'. Individual behaviour is increasingly free, but the role of parents remains important. McDonald's and trainers are ubiquitous, but the smallest spark reignites anti-American sentiment and a quest for Chinese authenticity. The voices most critical of government policies, and those who call most vigorously for freedom of the press and legal protection of 'vulnerable groups', can be, at the same time, opposed to parliamentary democracy.[9]

Secondly, modernisation theory is inoperative because it slices the social into autonomous spheres—spheres that, in China as elsewhere, happily overlap. Much more in accord with economic sociology,[10] or historical sociology,[11] than transitionalism in this respect, the Chinese economy is an arena where social relations, political conflicts, state logics, and imaginaries play a decisive role in defiance of pure, perfect competition. The law and its application is prey to political ambitions, projects of domination, friendships and enmities. The 'social' is not a particular domain, but the site where economic activities are generated and political strategies determined.[12]

Finally, modernisation theory is incapable of accounting for the complexity of the relations between individuals and society. The 'Chinese' are supposed to become autonomous individuals, released from the constraints of tradition and authoritarian power. In reality, China has not eluded the paradoxes of modern individualism, as analysed by Norbert Elias. Individualism has become a norm. One *must* be an autonomous, rational subject, a businessman motivated by self-interest, a citizen obliged to determine in his heart of hearts what is good for him and for the public good. In reality, however, this quest is never free of social determinants. Furthermore, if individuals distinguish themselves and exhibit character, they are also past masters in the art of manipulating the 'rules' of social existence and understanding which way the wind is blowing. The 'modern person', the 'hipster', the 'character', or 'freethinker' is just as much a product of socialisation—the prevalent practices, norms and values and their assimilation—as of 'individualisation'. They know how to manipulate signs.[13]

Today, it must be recognised that, notwithstanding their greater sophistication by comparison with the past, few analyses escape these two sources of inspiration. 'Democracy', the 'subject', the 'market' and the 'rule of law' are supposedly notions alien to the Chinese world. Even those who plump for the concord of civilisations, as opposed to their clash, start from the principle that there are two blocs—one Western, the other Chinese—which are, *a priori*, foreign to one another. Others believe that China's 'lag' in the transition is attributable to simple blockages (bound up with the preservation of a single party and totalitarian/bureaucratic logic), which disrupt its evolution towards modernity. By gradually learning Western norms, or via the convergence of universal norms, China will end up according with the '*ius commune*'.

A Critical Reflection

Readers will have understood that the aim of this book is not to provide an encyclopaedic tool intended to describe the major institutions—army, religion, party, and so on—or list the major social issues—unemployment, the role of women, the demography of contemporary China, and so forth. Nor does it seek to provide an overview of the different theories and trends underpinning knowledge of China. The approach proposed consists in analysing social reality—stratification, immediate or 'remote' social relations, the practices and imaginaries of individuals and groups, the power relationships mobilised in them—employing the tools of social science. It therefore does not involve starting from pre-established substances, but 'constructing' an object—the trajectory of Chinese society—on the basis of the phenomena, practices and representations that can be detected in it, without suppressing the paradoxes, contradictions and uncertainties which emerge, and without presuming the end-point of this trajectory.[14]

Chinese society will therefore be regarded here as a 'normal' society, whose seeming inconsistencies—unbridled capitalism and omnipresent state, frenzied individualism and blind obedience to collective rules, non-egalitarian social stratification and spectacular rise in living standards, a more democratic society and a 'monolithic' political system, citizens who protest but who are uninterested in changing the political regime—will have to be rendered intelligible by the analysis.

The task is enormous and immodest. Who could claim to account for French or English societies in a short book? So, Chinese society… I have had to make choices. Groups like ethnic minorities or dissidents, institutions like the army, the police and prison system, and important issues like demography, will not be tackled or only very briefly. This is bound to frustrate or irritate many readers. In particular, I have neglected what is most familiar to them (the one-child policy for example), and also what seemed to me least important—like the issue of national minorities[15]—to provide a global understanding of the trajectory of Chinese society. But does not doing social science involve prioritising phenomena so that the details do not make readers lose sight of the bigger picture? And does it not involve privileging what, at any given moment, seems most significant?

Given this, it seems problematic not to start with the historicity of contemporary society—that is, with the living, continually recreated traces of recent history (Chapter 1). Historicity does not refer here to the weight of an eternal history whose influence is supposedly diffuse and mysterious, but, on the contrary, to specific, perennial, still living practices that refer back, whether consciously or not, 'authentically' or otherwise, to past experience. These living memories are imagined but they have obvious impacts on people's practices.

In order to avoid drowning in the multitude of events that have marked the reform period, it will next be necessary to offer an overview of the changes undergone by Chinese society since the late 1980s (Chapter 2), and then to present the new lines of social stratification: the existing classes and groups, the decisive strategic resources, the new modes of social domination that have been established (Chapter 3).

One of the major questions that occurs with any social configuration, and which helps make it come alive for the reader, is the often mythologised relations between individual and society. How, amid the consumer society, free enterprise and the creation of personal lifestyles, is the individual's conformity ensured? How to be an individual in reformist China (Chapter 4)?

Finally, many observers contrast a dynamic economy and society with a static political sphere. But how, then, are we to reconcile the putative 'democratic deficit' of China with the climate of social unrest it is experiencing? All social milieus, or virtually all, are prey to strong protest movements. So what is the tenor of the complex relations between 'political power' and 'society'? Between the state and the various social categories, but also between the state and that fringe of the population—intellectuals, experts, researchers—which plays an important role both in deciding public policy and in protest movements, in criticising the 'system' and developing official discourse? Might we be able to shed light on the new modes of domination by comparing them with the trajectories of other social configurations?

It remains to clarify the sources I have relied on to write this book. In addition to the academic documentation (books, articles, theses, reports) generated by international research, I have made a great deal of use of the works of my Chinese colleagues. In particular, the teaching I did for six years in Tsinghua allowed me access to the very rich work of students and professors in the sociology department. My time in Beijing afforded me an opportunity to conduct many interviews and inquiries among different social categories. Finally, the Chinese press has become a source of highly valuable information, which I have drawn on widely.

1

HISTORICAL TRAJECTORY

The notion of 'historicity' enables us to avoid both the radicalism of 'historicism'—the view that past history completely
determines the present—and the pitfalls of modernisation
theory—societies supposedly follow a natural slope leading
them towards market democracy. It involves assessing the
impress of past experience and seeing how it is reused, integrated, manipulated and reinvented for the purposes of contemporary practices.[1]

This is a difficult issue to handle in the Chinese case, because
we are dealing with a society that is supposed to be 'ancient',
whereas it experienced the most spectacular upheavals during
the twentieth century. Hence, obviously, the temptation to
understand recent events and phenomena in the light of a 'tradition' or, conversely, to regard 1949 or 1979 as milestones in
a new era where past experiences and representations play but
a marginal role.

Before the Revolution[2]

In the late nineteenth century and first half of the twentieth
century, most Chinese remained peasants (three-quarters of the
workforce), were barely educated, and regarded the family as

the foundation of social existence. But which family? While in the south the clan—connected to a common ancestor—played an important role, everywhere else the restricted family was the norm. Yet things were far from stable. Unmarried people were common, while natural catastrophes, wars and poverty compelled whole families to abandon their village and even to emigrate.

Workers represented a tiny percentage of the population (2.5 million, or 0.5 per cent of the total) and remained strongly marked by their peasant origin. Nevertheless, if the village was a powerful locus of identity for them, and if the migrant workers who toiled in the major metropolises tended to recreate 'communities', this stemmed not from some 'familialism', but from the need to preserve or recreate bonds so as to survive in a hostile environment. Workers banded together by geographical origin to find a job in an embryonic labour market and to protect themselves against unscrupulous employers. Trade unions were marked by the peasant origin of their members, but they organised strikes and demonstrations.

Society was still based on 'the relative importance of landed wealth, Confucian knowledge and public service'.[3] The ruling class, a mix of merchants and men of letters, persisted. But while notables remained the masters of the countryside, we note an exodus to the towns and cities by 'big landowners'. Only small landowners and the stewards of large estates remained *in situ*. Finally, the life of most peasants was wretched and the concentration of land remained limited. Many people possessed small plots that enabled them just about to survive and compelled them to rent land or to labour as agricultural workers on other people's land. They fell into outright poverty at the slightest climatic, economic or military tremor.

Capitalism was weak, but it existed. It was introduced by foreigners, in its modern form at least. However, a national capitalism developed during the 'golden age' of the years 1912–27 and characteristic institutions, such as chambers of commerce, exercised an influence that was far from negligible. What posed a problem was the 'assimilation of the elites', whether bureaucratic, economic (merchants and new captains of industry), intellectual (men of letters), military (war lords), or those of the various regions. The Guomindang state would not succeed in amalgamating them and establishing a regime capable of imposing itself on foreign powers. This failure led some to choose the Communist or Western option, or even that of collaborating with Japan. We also note the emergence of a middle class (teachers, civil servants, doctors, engineers) in a few towns and cities. Education progressed and, above all, an incredible intellectual renaissance occurred. Western philosophy touched large fringes of an intelligentsia that sought to re-think China and its society. The concepts of nation, people, democracy, state, civilisation and Chinese identity were completely overhauled. Opinions varied widely, but they profoundly renewed the way that the Chinese viewed their past, present and future.[4]

Chinese society prior to 1949 was characterised by a strong feeling of insecurity among the population. Wars, poverty, and the erosion of regulatory systems led to the development of migration, criminality and instability in people's lives, and hence to a tightening of the bonds of community. In the countryside militias were set up to protect properties from brigands; workers banded together in groups from their home regions to survive in cities; foreigners in their concessions had to rely on criminal gangs to maintain order; political activists and refugees took refuge in the areas controlled by foreigners. As a consequence, the 'restoration of order' was one of the leitmotifs that contributed to the victory of the Communist Party and the establishment of the new regime.

The intellectual environment also changed dramatically. The new theories of socialism, communism, nationalism and capitalism became the most influential ideologies, especially as far as politics was concerned; none of them was able to impose its supremacy.

The experience of insecurity and dramatic changes suffered by the country again in the late 1950s and during the Cultural Revolution, and which is re-emerging today in a different form, is therefore not unprecedented in Chinese history. The fear of disorder is part of pre-socialist Chinese society's traumatic baggage. It is also worth recalling that this society could no longer be considered as 'traditional' in its structures. In its recent history, China has already had a bourgeoisie, a middle class, and already experienced a period of intellectual cosmopolitanism, even if several generations have passed and, in the interim, Maoism obscured the history. These references to a recent past, whose experience and memories are, as it were, 'in a direct line'—of the order of a few generations—and therefore particularly pregnant, are frequently neglected in analyses of Chinese society. People prefer to refer to a remote antiquity, to the thinking of an author who has been dead for two and a half millennia, and whose books were written a few centuries later. Or, people prefer to evoke the emergence of an entirely new figure—the modern Chinese—keen on reason, freedom and fanatical individualism, but up against the forces of reaction. How can we ignore the fact that the quinquagenarians of the 2010s were wholly raised and formed in a socialist culture and their parents in a period of unparalleled upheaval?

A Grey Page[5]

The seizure of power by the Communist Party resulted in extensive destruction of the structure of Chinese society for the first half of the twentieth century. Landowners, 'bourgeois', and 'petit bourgeois' disappeared, if not physically, then as social groups, more or less rapidly and more or less violently. The stratification that derived from this upheaval is officially defined by the co-existence of two classes (workers and peasants) and a social stratum (intellectuals). Regardless of the self-evident facts, no ruling class is to be found in this schema, and nor is there an 'enemy' class, because the triumph of the Revolution could not tolerate such realities. Certainly, intellectuals did not form part of the people and, from the late 1950s, an attempt was made to manufacture 'black categories' plotting against the Party. However, this was a question of 'rekindling' the flame of the Revolution by inventing counter-revolutionaries.

The desire to make China a 'blank' page was nevertheless to run into serious difficulties. First of all, difficulties bound up with the regime's fluctuating objectives and the diversity of the policies adopted. There were fundamental differences between the desire to strengthen the country's power and prosperity by guaranteeing the population a certain standard of living—the objective of most of the 1950s—and the totalitarian ambitions of the Great Leap Forward or the Cultural Revolution. In both cases, of course, we note an obsession with public order, a desire to ensure extensive, profound control over the population's behaviour and opinions, and supervision of intellectual and artistic output. Some institutions, like 'reform through labour', which sought to 'change thinking', persisted throughout the period. The army would remain a pillar of the regime. Even so, the struggle between two lines, pitting those for whom the purpose of social control was to ensure economic growth and national power against those for whom total domination of 'souls' was an end in itself, made the creation of a new social order difficult.

A second factor of uncertainty stemmed from economic failures that discredited the regime. The catastrophe of the Great

Leap Forward was the decisive element in disaffection with the regime. More generally, we might note that inconsistency in economic policy resulted in an impasse. China drifted between integration into the Soviet bloc, opening up to the capitalist world, an auto-centred model of development, and radical anti-economism. The political and social chaos of the last period (1966–79) paralysed the economy. From the standpoint of the great majority of the population, the regime was synonymous with privation and insecurity.[6]

Finally, the authorities had to reckon with the population's ability to 'produce' social relations in response, which were outside or even inconsistent with the institutions of control. These new forms of solidarity were more than forms of 'resistance'; they gradually constituted veritable kernels of power undermining and rivalling the structures of social control.[7]

The 'stratification' of society

In the 1950s, the population was almost completely transformed into an army of stratified workers. Workers, teachers, office clerks and civil servants were combined in vast public 'work units' (*danwei*) and the rural population rapidly lost its autonomy, becoming paid wage-labourers in a system of 'work points' awarded according to their contribution.

At the bottom of the scale were the peasants. In all areas—economic, educational, social and, obviously, symbolic—they occupied the bottom of the social pyramid. Income differentials were certainly narrow, with urban dwellers earning just 1.3 times more than peasants in the late 1970s (as opposed to 3.13 times more in 2011). Nevertheless, in the towns and cities people were better fed, better clothed, better cared for, and had greater access to public facilities and leisure activities than in rural areas. Even in the richest villages, the gap with urban areas remained wide in virtually all domains.

The second class was that of 'workers and employees' (*zhigong*), comprising the workforce of public enterprises and government departments, or 78 per cent of total urban employment in 1978. This status involved the work unit's complete assumption of responsibility for the individual, from the first day of employment to the grave. *Zhigong*, who were allocated work bureaucratically and often arbitrarily—an arbitrariness tempered by the possibility of resorting to good personal relations—enjoyed a whole set of formal or informal privileges—a job for life, complete social security, social advantages for children, free housing, priority employment of family members, and so on—which increasingly widened the gap with peasants in terms of living standards. Furthermore, public enterprise being a significant political actor in the overall architecture of power relations, some of its prestige rubbed off on its employees. Finally, the latter could exploit the relational resources afforded by employment in a sizeable work unit. By these means, people were able to procure scarce goods or exchange services that were unavailable elsewhere. Affiliation to a faction or support for a cadre or foreman in his bureaucratic ascent could bring material advantages and social promotion—promotion that was certainly limited (generally in the same enterprise), but which, in a very rigid context, was all the more significant. In short, employees and workers formed a kind of socialist middle class, supposed to represent the quintessence of the 'people', the pillar of the regime and the future of the whole population.[8]

The 'intellectual stratum' comprised a group of individuals (artists, writers, thinkers, journalists) who were ill-situated socially and, above all, closely monitored by the authorities. Not members of the 'people', they were perceived as having an antagonistic position but were tolerated at a political price, which varied according to the epoch. In politically calm periods, they merely had to maintain a simple but scrupulous conformity with Party policy in their writings. In troubled times, however, the very status of intellectual became infamous and exposed people to all sorts of dangers.[9]

Classes that were not classes

Although defined as a simple group of officials included with the peasants and workers and obliged to 'serve the people' (*wei renmin fuwu*), cadres (*ganbu*) nevertheless constituted a *de facto* social class. The title was commonly used to refer to those possessing power, whether in enterprises, government departments or educational establishments. It involved a status very strictly organised into grades, each of which corresponded to a level of remuneration, fringe benefits, authority and prestige. Promotion went with seniority, but also with the vagaries of the political struggle, purges, and hence the fate of the cliques to which everyone was obliged to belong.

Here we must add another category of people—the 'enemies of the regime'—to be found in nearly all social groups (including the cadres during purges), which comprised individuals of 'bad social origin': those from landowning families, capitalists or members of the Guomindang and its army, people of Sino-foreign origin, and even, at times, graduates of foreign universities. They formed a kind of sub-proletariat, sometimes criminalised by the authorities, which was to be found on the margins of society, sometimes in prison or a camp, sometimes in more or less extended detention, and often doing dangerous and hard jobs.[10]

PSEUDO-EQUALITY BETWEEN THE SEXES

If there is one area where Maoist propaganda proved particularly effective, it was in getting people to believe that China had succeeded in ensuring well-nigh perfect equality between men and women. Certainly, thanks to the marriage law of 1950, women secured the same rights as men. Women's rate of participation in the workforce increased and wives were theoretically protected against bad treatment by their husbands and mothers-in-law.

Nevertheless, various works have shown that in rural areas, notwithstanding certain advances, society remained highly patriarchal. More recently, studies have revealed deep inequalities in the sphere of work. Participation has grown, but has always remained far below that of men. Moreover, while it increased in periods of labour shortages (the policy of major public works during the Great Leap Forward), it declined just as abruptly in phases of job shedding. In other words, women play the role of adjustment variable: many of them stopped working in the late 1970s, passing their jobs on to their sons.

It must also be pointed out that women do the lowest paid, hardest and least prestigious jobs. They are over-represented among temporary or non-statutory workers. They scarcely benefit from professional training within enterprises and are second to men when it comes to promotion. Finally, very few of them hold positions of power and, when they do, their functions are 'social'—trade union duties, for example—and hence relatively marginal.

It is also the case that sharing domestic labour was far from being the rule in the Maoist era, including in urban areas. Preparing meals, housework and childcare remained primarily female tasks.[11]

The resources of social stratification

The stratification of socialist China was established in accordance with a stable ideological and political framework, even if the weighting of different resources evolved over three decades of socialism. The dominant resource was obviously political in kind. Occupying a dominant position in the Party, state or public enterprise apparatus conferred prestige, power and, consequently, a set of material advantages. Social capital was another resource, intrinsically linked to the first. Having an important person in one's family, or somehow 'knowing' one, brought privileges. Finally, social and family origin, by classifying individuals, situated them in higher or lower positions in the social hierarchy. The fate of individuals was completely different depending on whether their parents were classified as poor peasants or landowners.

Accumulation on a personal basis being impossible, economic capital played no role. The only way of accessing certain goods was to exploit the privileges afforded by a certain position in the social hierarchy. As for the possession of cultural credentials, it was a source of some prestige when economic growth and expertise were sought after and of great inconvenience in periods of totalitarian high intensity.

Differences of condition between social strata, and within strata, were limited. The average city-dweller never went beyond a state of 'dignified poverty'. He or she ate their fill, but it was nourishment without any refinement, containing very little meat and very little variety (in the north, mounds of cabbage were replaced in summer by mounds of watermelons).

Strictly speaking, there were no rich peasants and poor peasants, but a relatively well-off tiny minority living for the most part in model villages and a mass of peasants who were impoverished to varying degrees. Similarly, the difference in living standards between employees and workers was mainly limited to the possession of a bicycle and access to a few scarce goods.

Employment was a right and workers were state employees. Urban workers were allocated to an enterprise in the context of a policy of expanding the wage-earning class, although wages were not performance-based. The wage was an income determined by a job and grade that possessed no economic function, particularly as regards consumption. On the contrary, in order to be able to employ the whole population, it was necessary 'to keep wages low to create jobs' (*di gongzi, duo jiu*). In economic exchange, all the individual's needs were catered for by the work units.[12]

With the notorious exception of a few very senior leaders, the material privileges of cadres came down at best to use of a car, a spacious flat, and access to certain consumer goods. Such differences were significant and categorised individuals, but were ultimately on a small scale. The worker and cadre remained, as it were, part of the same world. Furthermore, material privileges were bound up with a post and did not belong to the person holding it. If they lost this post, they lost everything.

The scale of social inequality was strictly limited by the impossibility of publicly displaying its symbols. 'Distinction' had to be discreet. Everyone knew that society was not egalitarian, but differences in condition had to remain discreet. Thus, enjoyment of privileges was a wholly personal thing that did not thrive on self-display in front of others. The curtains of official cars (the famous limousine-type *hongqi*) were drawn. Parties were private; consumption was never conspicuous. Even the slightest show of originality, whether sartorial, dietary, corporeal or discursive, was strongly discouraged, and sometimes strictly prohibited—and this right up to the summit of the state. We know of the frustration of the last Madame Mao at not being able to wear a dress in public and the big trouble the wife of Prime Minister Liu Shaoqi brought upon herself by appearing elegantly dressed at official receptions. Overall, the dominant style was worker/peasant, comprising simplicity or even asceticism and contempt for proprieties and politeness. People belched, farted, and ate messily and loudly. This style, which contrasted with a very strict control of instincts, desires, feelings and speech, persists today among most of those aged fifty and over, even though things are gradually changing. Such standardisation of tastes and ways of living affected all social categories. On this score there was little difference between peasants, workers, cadres and intellectuals.

A society of estates

Socialist China was a society of 'statuses' or 'estates', in the sense that the position of individuals was determined by factors over which they had little control. People 'belonged' to a status and these statuses were transmissible. Parents of 'bad class origin' conferred that infamous rubric on their children, while the offspring of 'workers' or 'poor peasants' immediately formed part of the 'people'. Moreover, the new regime legalised and objectified the city–countryside divide. Spontaneous migration was impossible. Peasants did not have the right to work in towns or to reside there. Some of them—mainly peasants from suburban regions—came to swell the ranks of the working class in the first half of the 1950s; some were subsequently 'repatriated', but in small numbers and in the framework of controlled migration. All the rest suffered legal and social discrimination that confined them to their village for life. Their economic role was to produce a surplus, which the state absorbed in its entirety to industrialise the country.

The residence system (*hukou*), established in the 1950s, fixed every individual in their birthplace. People did not have the right to leave it, even temporarily, without authorisation from the relevant authorities. Trips had to be justified by specific professional or family reasons (studies, business trips, meetings). Only transfer to another city or, more rarely, marriage provided an opportunity for a change of residence. Control was reinforced by the rationing that lasted until the 1980s. Tickets for the principal foodstuffs and certain durable goods were valid solely in the place of issue. Tickets for other durable goods—bikes, for example—were delivered by the work unit. Finally, despite the professed wish to implement strict equality between men and women, sex largely determined destiny. In the countryside, the patriarch remained the family head even if women had their own wage. In the towns, not all women worked—far from it.

In urban areas, control by residence was further strengthened by the institution of residents' committees, whose members were theoretically chosen by the inhabitants of each residential area (when the district was distinct from the work unit) but in reality were selected by local Party bodies. They monitored everyone's doings very closely and represented a first line of social control.

Mass organisations—trade unions, the Women's Federation, the Young Communist League, the Student Federation, and so forth—supervised each of the social categories, represented them, and mobilised them around political slogans and activity decided by the Party.

As a result, social reproduction was very pronounced. Children inherited not only the political status of their parents, but also their place of residence and often their profession. The offspring of peasants were peasants in the village of their parents or, in the case of females, in that of their husband. In cities, the socialisation of children and professional training were in part undertaken by work units, and employees' children often became apprentices in them. Endogamy was widespread, not out of 'custom', but simply because the restriction of social existence to a narrow space offered no other prospect. People married in the neighbouring village, or within their work unit, or thanks to matchmaking by a colleague.

In these circumstances, opportunities for social mobility scarcely existed. A (limited) improvement in living standard or social status generally occurred in the same enterprise and went with seniority. For a peasant to become a worker was exceptional; and opportunities to improve one's standard of living were extremely rare. A worker of good social origin could become a cadre, but this presupposed political activism in Party bodies and trade unions and, above all, taking risks. The ambitious could support a political patron so as to climb the social ladder quicker, but his fall entailed theirs.[13]

New Solidarities: Towns and Cities

The Mao period is often seen as an era of destruction, which is true. To varying degrees, and depending on region and period, religions and religious buildings, families, social groups and individuals suffered considerable harm. Yet the urge to destroy social relations and penetrate the innermost core of the individual, albeit totalitarian or authoritarian, was also creative. It created new social groups and new social relations, some of which were desired by the regime, while others formed outside of it. We must reckon with the unanticipated consequences of phenomena, policies or events like the Great Leap Forward.

It was the socialist state that created the Chinese working class. The number of workers in the secondary sector reached 15 million in 1952 and nearly 74 million in 1978. Officially, the working class was 'master' (*zhurenweng*) of the country. In reality, it was under the heel of the class of cadres while forming the social base of the regime, a privileged group. The link between the dominant class and workers was therefore based not on exploitation of labour, but on a form of domination/dependence that conditioned both workers' working and living conditions and forms of protest. The collective actions of Chinese workers did not challenge exploitation. Some were reactions against the abolition of material advantages hitherto guaranteed by the administrative status of 'worker and employee'. Others involved categories of state worker (apprentices, temporary employees), or workers in collective enterprises, whose pay and working conditions were inferior to the norm.

Such conflicts were generally settled within the bureaucracy as an administrative problem, with the official trade union playing the role of intermediary, at once conveyer belt and echo chamber of working-class discontent. Even when mass demands outflanked institutions, protest remained confined to status. During the Hundred Flowers movement, and especially the Cultural Revolution, it was not the capital/labour relationship that was subject to challenge but hierarchical relationships and the regime's conformity to its principles. In particular, many people were questioning the fact that cadres had more power and better living conditions than the country's masters.[14]

However, confinement to enclosed spaces—work unit, district, village, social category—which was intended to isolate individuals and thereby control them more firmly, paradoxically created new kinds of identity and helped to create solid bonds of solidarity between individuals. 'Workers and employees' strongly identified with their status. A symbol of the regime's social successes, they were represented as the healthiest part of society: neither backward peasants nor unproductive cadres, they were positioned at the heart of the development of the socialist economy. Moreover, urban residents inhabited ghettos. They worked, lived, and entertained themselves with a

25

very small number of individuals, who were always the same. Often their children went to school with the children of their colleagues and immediate neighbours, and no newcomers arrived to disrupt the life of these small, self-contained groups. The exclusiveness and intensity of relations induced a strong sense of solidarity. Similarly, often pursuing all or part of their career in the same unit, those in charge were led to defend its interests: they too belonged to small groups. Obviously, there was no question of relying on these relations of solidarity between cadres and employees to challenge directives from the centre. But it was possible to implement them while seeking, so far as possible, to eliminate their potentially harmful consequences for the individuals for whom the cadre was responsible. This 'particularism' made it possible to preserve a minimum of social peace despite the continuous political campaigns that were supposed to re-launch the revolution in behaviour.

New Solidarities: The Countryside

Social life in villages was profoundly transformed by the new regime. The collectivisation of the land and labour in the framework of people's communes challenged relations of domination based on wealth, seniority and patriarchy. Not all regions had known the same type of social organisation, but in all of them power was in the hands of men who had wealth and education. The new regime socially destroyed the class of landowners and physically destroyed many of its members.

Most peasants were reduced to a middling condition of rural wage-labourer. The elderly and males thus lost the economic basis of their power. Land, capital, and even personal goods in some periods, were no longer bequeathed from generation to generation and thus no longer represented a means of domination over the young, who had to await the death or debility of the elderly in order to become dominant in their turn. Even if wages were paid directly to the family, both youth and women now had their own 'wage', in the form of work points that they accumulated on performance of the various tasks allocated to them. The 'social protection' of people unable to work was no longer ensured by the family, but by the state. Everyone acquired a social existence of their own. At the same time, most of the popular cults that contributed to the solidarity of family, clan or village organisations were destroyed or forced underground.

Nevertheless, the new setup did not entirely meet the radical objectives of the rulers. While peasants were generally impoverished, the project of a complete equalisation of conditions was a failure. Poverty varied with the location of regions and the social status of individuals. Status depended on social origin—landowners, rich, middle or poor peasants—and each person's relations (or lack of relations) with those wielding power. The elderly and men partly retained their dominant position. Relatives remained united, as attested both by the pursuit of vendettas and the maintenance of mutual aid among members of the same family. At the same time, the project of creating a new man, completely controlled by the Party and without emotional ties, experienced serious reverses. The cadres in charge of collectivisation bodies did not fail to favour their relatives, friends and 'clients' when it came to assigning tasks, securing advantages, or making promotions. 'Localism' assumed a new salience on account of the policy of making the countryside autonomous. Like peasants, leaders favoured the interests of villages and different administrative entities and had to find ways both to obey orders from above and to satisfy at least a section of the local population. Moreover, the almost constant changes in policy and internal struggles rendered the role highly unstable. The need to escape purges and support political movements without suffering a backlash made Chinese cadres experts in shams and fake relations, delaying actions, and scheming. Only the least shrewd, or most unlucky, succumbed. The rest developed the ability to decode official texts, guess the intentions of superiors, and negotiate in order to handle policies from above and actors on the ground.

UTOPIA AND MASSACRES

The seemingly irrational aspect of many political decisions represents one of the main difficulties in analysing the Maoist period. Thus, the self-sufficiency of the Great Leap Forward can partly be explained by the problems of dependency created by anchorage in the Soviet bloc, and by the Party's difficulties in mobilising and controlling the population. But its excesses—over-exploitation of labour, neglect of agricultural work in favour of rural industrialisation, ultra-collectivisation, and so on—and the loss of any grasp of reality by some leaders, refer us to a mystical-millenarian way of thinking. Another example: the Cultural Revolution, which was a kind of popular revolution by decree that set the whole country ablaze, pitting children against parents, young against old, ruled against rulers, to enable a few leaders to maintain their dictatorial power. Finally, the utopian desire to change man reached a peak in 'thought reform', to which alleged or real enemies of the regime were subjected. The objective was not simply to make individuals obey, but to change them completely, to track down their bad thoughts to their innermost being, to convince them that they were wrong. We have never been as close to Orwell's *1984* as in some periods of Maoism.

In the final reckoning, the human cost of such political movements and repression was colossal. Over and above the friendships, relationships and families destroyed, and the physical and mental suffering, the figures quoted are overwhelming. Twenty to forty million deaths are cited for the Great Leap Forward, 20 million for the 'Chinese gulag', and 1 million for the Cultural Revolution.[15]

Even the industrialisation of the countryside, intended to ensure the autarky of villages and hence eliminate the last vestiges of commercial capitalism, had unanticipated consequences. New modes of work and management were to emerge; paradoxically, some villages and townships were to experience more activity in trading, transport and production than in the past. These new skills would be very helpful when the future reforms created new business opportunities.

The Tragic Failure of Totalitarianism

The project of complete control of social relations by the Party-State ended in failure—a tragic failure. Tragic, because the repression of the early 1950s, the anti-rightist movement of 1957, the Great Leap Forward, and the Cultural Revolution resulted in the death and imprisonment of tens of millions of people. A failure, above all, because the new man never emerged. In his stead, new social relations developed both in the interstices of the mechanisms of domination and within them. They did not escape 'power', but were slotted into it and exploited it where possible. Families continued to help one another; office and factory colleagues exchanged services; friendships were preserved or formed; cadres maintained a network of clients. These links sometimes played a decisive role. Young graduates sent into the countryside survived thanks to the help of local peasants or the mutual aid of their peers; and, once, they secretly returned home in the late 1970s, thanks to family and kin networks. Once their parents came back to power at the beginning of the 1970s, the children and 'clients' of senior cadres enjoyed again significant privileges. The benefits, mostly in kind, which workers (and, more rarely, peasants) might enjoy depended less on the possession of particular talents or a greater capacity for work, than on harmonious

29

relations with a particular category of the dominant: local cadres and foremen.

From the start of the 1980s, such social relations, situated both inside and outside the system, were to become the main vectors through which individuals had access to the opportunities for social mobility and economic diversification provided by the reforms.

2

THE LONG MARCH OF REFORMS

As happened during the French Revolution, and in a number of authoritarian regimes with high ideological ambitions (Cambodia, Iran, Vietnam, etc.), China made a transition from 'Terror' to 'Thermidor'.[1] In other words, the revolutionary elites abandoned their demiurgic objectives of transforming society in its entirety by force. They did not renounce changing China and restoring its power, but adopted different methods. Henceforth it would be necessary to take heed of society and refashion it, but with it, not against it. Priority would now be given to the virtue of compromising with interests and desires. Less reference would be made to ideological and political principles than to a rapid, tangible improvement in living standards, an increase in food supplies, the prosperity of a significant part of the population, security and social mobility. Since the end of the 1970s, China has experienced what Hannah Arendt termed the 'rise of the social',[2] in which everything is perceived in terms of production, consumption, income and exchange. Activities that were restricted to the household sphere and linked to the necessities of life have become the main topics of public discussion. The rise of the social is also characterised by the growing importance of bureaucratic administration, which manages the economy and all aspects of social life (education, social protection, etc).

It will be many years yet before we can furnish readers with a detailed analysis of the reasons for the reforms. However, we must rule out the seductive idea that they began with a fully worked-out project and an established (eventually reproducible) model. The history of the reforms is full of hesitations, retreats and sudden spurts, followed by periods of stagnation. In this process, chance and the unanticipated consequences of seemingly anodyne policies must be given their due. Chinese reform was a series of actions based on 'guess work', which depended on the unfolding of events.

As to the decisive factor, there is no doubt that it is to be sought in the conjunction of two circumstances. On the one hand, the action of a political class that was bruised, wearied and disorientated by thirty years of 'revolution' but still well organised and integrated and sharing a common bureaucratic culture. On the other hand, the disenchantment of a society that was poor and exhausted, and which no longer conferred much legitimacy on its rulers but which was, at the same time, well educated, well trained but deprived of decent living conditions. The struggle between a permanent revolution conducted by a small group of tyrants dreaming of total control of individuals and less 'ambitious' leaders, ready to come to terms with social reality, was not new. However, in the last years of Maoist rule it took a more radical turn. Rather like the French Revolution, the Chinese Revolution devoured itself through successive, violent purges of leaders and cadres; and the dominant class clearly wanted to ensconce itself, stabilise its rule, rationalise its power, and professionalise itself. The population was equally desirous of a more predictable, less wretched world. The undermining of the apparatus of control consequent upon factional struggles resulted in a certain *de facto* autonomy of particular social categories. Educated youth returned to the towns legally or illegally and proved difficult to manage. Criminality re-emerged. Peasants spontaneously decollectivised 'their' land and some leaders allowed this to happen. There was a very real risk of the whole population 'defecting'.

But it would be wrong to regard the switch to reform as a sheer instrumentalisation of discontent by elites at bay or the conversion of the elites to the benefits of economic rationality. The aim was always to make China a prosperous and powerful nation. Similarly, it would be incorrect to say that the revolutionary spirit completely disappeared from the scene. First of all, because the ruling class and a significant percentage of the population were trained in the school of the Revolution: preservation of the ritualisation of political life and constant attachment to order are proof of this. Next, because China officially remains a socialist country mindful of the 'people': we are not dealing with reversion to a pre-revolutionary regime. Finally, because 'modernisation' is itself a revolutionary project and accords with the rhetoric of national independence, the restoration of Chinese 'greatness', and the struggle against archaisms by promoters of a new China since the nineteenth century. Were the abrupt de-collectivisation of the land, the one-child policy, and the opening of capitalist enclaves not revolutionary policies in the context of the 1970s and 1980s? As for the liquidation of socialist industry, it stunned all those observers who believed at the time—the mid-1990s—that the regime would never survive a plunge into the sea of capitalism. Everyone thought that converting to capitalism automatically involved a change of political regime and a profound transformation of the elites.

The pursuit of 'revolution' by other means nevertheless led to two paradoxes that encapsulate everything at stake in the reforms. Abroad, it involved China adapting to the world the better to assert itself as a power with its own cultural and political peculiarities. At home, modernisation involved changes that risked endangering stability and, consequently, the growth it was supposed to stimulate. Consequently, the authorities never seriously envisaged a genuinely liberal policy as regards social control. The repressive apparatus has remained in place 'in case', even though, from the late 1990s, it has been employed sparingly and gradually relaxed.

The Mutual Formation of the State and Market

The method used by the Chinese Thermidorian elites is a 'default' model. It involves releasing entrepreneurial energies (whether individual and familial or factional and clientelist) while maintaining social and political stability. It therefore entails great disparities, because there is no question of radically challenging social hierarchy. The privileges granted to some regions (the special economic zones) or to some people (those in the cities have better access to education) have created inequalities, while the regions that were already "rich" (in raw materials, local goods, road infrastructure, educational levels, etc.) have been advantaged. Powerful families and cliques have used their networks to benefit from reform policy. Enjoying greater access to education, urban residents are in a position to monopolise well-paid jobs. In brief, the social stratification inherited from the past constitutes the environment on which people have to rely so as to display their entrepreneurial talents.

Social capital, accumulated by affiliations created in the Maoist era, is becoming an essential resource for success. People often mock the disproportionate role immediately assumed by networks of relations (*guanxi wang*) in reformist China, at the expense of meritocratic rules and selection by the market. But there is nothing cultural about this. The vacuum left by the break-up of socialist planning was spontaneously filled by recourse to personal relationships. Individuals, enterprises and social groups with substantial relational capital were to occupy a prominent position. As for markets, they were not formed against networks of relations but, on the contrary, by gradually being grafted onto them.[3]

Cautiously at the outset, the reforms set about dismantling whatever might hobble initiative and the free play of interests—price controls, the prohibition of migration, legal limits to enterprise, the closing of borders, obstacles to workforce mobility, class labels—without placing China under the auspices of a pure, perfect market and without changing social stratification. On the one hand, because the state retained a clear wish to control and organise the market and, on the other, because the market recreated monopolies in and of itself: it enabled the most powerful to impose their rules. In other words, China tested out what other countries had already experienced: the development of capitalism, which assumes the action and formation—sometimes combined, and sometimes conflictual, but invariably mutual—of the state and the market.[4] In China, as elsewhere, the interplay between these two entities is not a zero sum game; what is won by the market is not lost by the state, because the latter sees its power increased by economic success. Conversely, if the state's operations become more efficient and extend to new areas, the institutionalisation of the market will emerge strengthened.

In this major development, two phases can be distinguished. The first began at the end of the 1970s and ended with the Tiananmen Square events. It was characterised by a degree of prudence. The second began during Deng Xiaoping's 'trip to the south' in 1992 and gave pride of place to more radical reforms, which challenged the legacy of the socialist epoch more profoundly.

Table 1: Basic Data

Years	1978	2012
Total population	962 million	1,354 million
Rural population	82.08%	47.4%
Urban population	17.92%	52.6%

Source: *Chinese Statistical Yearbook 2009*; *internet site of the National Bureau of Statistics*

A Marginal Capitalism (1978–91)

As in Polanyi's description of the development of capitalism in Western Europe in the nineteenth and twentieth centuries, the Chinese variant has taken the form of a commodification of the land, capital and labour. Nevertheless, China's specificities emerged fairly rapidly, in particular as regards a very moderate liberalisation. It was not the land that was privatised, but only its exploitation. Peasants only enjoyed rights of usufruct over agricultural cultivation. The state retained its stranglehold on the commercialisation of most raw materials and all of the banking system, while the commodification of labour was limited because state workers kept their status and migration remained restricted until the end of the 1990s.[5] In this initial phase of post-Maoist China, the foundations of social stratification were therefore not challenged. The reforms remained circumspect. Capitalism was introduced on the margins of a society that remained mostly socialist. New social categories emerged, but they only occupied a very small part of the social space.[6]

The maintenance of structures

The very first thing we note is the preservation of the legal and social dualism differentiating the rural population from the urban population. The residence system (*huji zhidu*) continued to fix people in their place of birth or where they worked. Certainly, the population began to move but not in great numbers and not far away. Peasants in suburban areas were authorised to come and sell their output in towns and even to stay there on a temporary basis. Some migrants were employed in newly founded special economic zones factories and rural enterprises but job opportunities were limited, especially for those who were not locals. The decollectivisation of the land, trade liberalisation, and price increases decided by the authorities resulted in a significant rise in peasant living standards. Peasants now had great leeway as regards output, work organisation and, to a certain extent, marketing their harvest. Some began to specialise in industrial crops or to set up enterprises, notably in transport. Even so, the fate of the peasantry did not change radically. From the mid-1980s, peasant incomes began to decline compared with those of urban residents. In the towns and cities, the supply of jobs remained weak and illegal migrants felt the impact of restrictive policies. Some professions were reserved for the urban population and the police conducted round-ups to repatriate undesirables.[7] The rural population did not benefit from the return to normality in the education system. Likewise, social segregation vis-à-vis peasants was maintained, and even accentuated, on account of the new opportunities rural dwellers had been given to move. Farmers coming to sell their output were held responsible for the inflation that was rife at the time. They were also suspected of taking 'the jobs of town folk'. Their behaviour, deemed uncultured and boorish (*tu*), their way of life, regarded as 'primitive', and their alleged dirtiness made them a repellent category.

A second element of continuity was the system of work units. Enterprises underwent a set of reforms. Contractualisation of the workforce, financial and managerial autonomy, and price liberalisation led to an introduction of the categories of the market economy. Nevertheless, resistance emerged. Resistance from employees, even enterprise managers, evinced unease about the consequences of possible or probable policy U-turns.[8] The Cultural Revolution was a recent memory and there was no proof that the reforms would last: what would happen if one were too clearly in favour of something resembling 'capitalism'? Undue support for 'bourgeois' reforms risked costing very dear. Moreover, if everyone, whether employee or bureaucrat, rejoiced at the positive impact of the reforms on their living standards, they were hardly favourable to any challenge to their established rights. If contractualisation of the wage-earning class opened the door to potential rises in income, it threatened jobs for life. If enterprise cadres gained more managerial power, they could also lose it because of the enhanced power of the role of 'experts' (accountants, engineers, salespersons), whose skills were indispensable to the development of enterprises. In short, people wanted to earn more, but certainly not to see their benefits imperilled.

In fact, far from diminishing, the number of employees and workers in public enterprises continued to grow over the period, rising from 74 million in 1978 to 112 million in 1994, and enterprises were incapable of increasing labour productivity. They even saw their income rise with the introduction of methods of remuneration aimed at stimulating workers' activity, although inflation wiped out a significant percentage of the gains. Still enjoying many privileges in terms of social protection, they preserved their status of socialist 'middle class'.

Finally, the political personnel remained in place. The new enterprises, whether private or mixed, were under the control of the state. Public enterprises were still directed by bureaucrats of the old or new generation, even if reference began to be made to training, competition and recruitment on the basis of people's skills and to excluding the bureaucracy from direct management of the economy.[9]

Some ruptures

The first rupture involved the abandonment of use of 'class labels' to categorise individuals. Not only did individuals and families of 'bad origin' lose their infamous status, but they often staged a notable return to the social scene: major capitalist families re-employed as advisers to a Prince keen for advice on a world of which he was ignorant; trading families whose *savoir-faire* once again found a use. More generally, the end of class labels opened up new prospects for the whole population. Social origin now no longer represented, as it were, an official obstacle to social mobility. 'Estates' disappeared and were replaced by social status as the main element of social classification.

The second rupture affected education. From the second half of the 1970s, universities once again operated normally. Studying became an activity that was not only legitimate, but also necessary to succeed.

The third rupture concerned the legitimation of non-public enterprises. By this term is intended private, mixed, family, etc. enterprises, which emerged on the margins of the public sector. In rural areas, the development of township and village enterprises (*xiangzhen qiye*) enabled the on-site commodification of the labour of part of the surplus rural population. Created during the Great Leap Forward, rural enterprises saw their workforce rise from 30 million in 1980 to 123 million in 1993. Some were private, while others were set up by local authorities. But they all enjoyed the benefits of the interpenetration of the political and the economic, which made it possible to take advantage of the market, and of proximity to power (access to raw materials, transport networks, administrative authorisation).[10] We also observe the emergence of capitalist enclaves located on the southern coast (special economic zones and other 'development zones'), which enjoyed legal facilities for attracting capital, creating jobs and, above all, accessing new technology. Guangdong and Fujian were the two flagship provinces of this sector, which was mainly export-orientated. This was the start of the emergence of a new working class composed of peasants (the *nongmingong*), who were to become the drudges of the Chinese 'miracle'. At the time, it was simply a question, in specific places, of temporarily allowing a small proportion of the rural population, often settled on the periphery of towns, to earn money before returning home and (it was hoped) stimulating local growth thanks to their investments and recently acquired *savoir-faire*. In 2012, their total numbered 236 million and many were *de facto* urban residents.

Finally, in the towns and cities capitalism was introduced via different channels. On the one hand, we witness the emergence of private enterprises (*siying qiye*) and urban sham collective enterprises—formally affiliated to public bodies—where working conditions were fairly similar to those commonly found in the capitalist 'enclaves'. Small in size, they only employed a very limited number of workers. On the other hand, a set of small-scale commercial activities developed, grouped under the rubric of individual sector (*geti*). The individual entrepreneur generally only employed his family and, less frequently, a few employees.[11] The final capitalist margin involved the new modern sector that arose on the ruins of the old public economy. From the mid-1980s, companies (*gongsi*) created by government departments in sectors where profits were particularly lucrative flourished: tourism, the hotel industry, trade in raw materials, transport, finance, and so forth. These are the ancestors of the monopoly groups that were gradually constructed in the 1990s.[12] Via them, the bureaucrats were gradually initiated into the mysteries of business.

CHINESE SOURCES AND STATISTICS

The social sciences rely not only on methods, but also sources of information. In the case of China, data collection long remained sparse. As with any totalitarian system, we have to be cautious with statistics because of their use in propaganda. Political struggle is also a battle of figures: it was imperative to be best not only in comparison with capitalist countries, but also the neighbouring district. Alongside this general reality, a marked feature of China is its administrative decentralisation. To obtain data, Beijing had no alternative but to tot up the figures supplied from below, without much possibility of controlling them. As for works facilitating a qualitative appreciation of social reality, they were virtually non-existent prior to the reforms. The 'Leninisation' of social science research between 1949 and 1966 was followed by its disappearance until the start of the 1980s. These facts oblige today's researcher to reconstruct the events and phenomena of the Maoist years from a distance. Certainly, some archives have been opened, retrospective statistics published, and documents rediscovered. But on many subjects, and for numerous periods, testimony and memory remain the primary source.

The situation is much better today. Statistics are plentiful, fieldwork encounters few obstacles, and the publications of Chinese researchers are generally of good quality.[13] We have made considerable use of them here. Even so, there is still much imprecision. The nomenclature of professions has not been standardised; local statistics are often fanciful. In the *China Statistical Yearbook*, different figures are given for the same category, without any explanation being offered for such discrepancies. Cross-checking of sources, or the use of estimates gleaned from interviews, is often the only way of filling these lacunae and yet one still often emerges frustrated.

A Hesitant Stratification

All in all, social stratification only changed moderately in these years. 'Social origin' lost any 'legal' value, but the existing social determinations continue to disadvantage or advantage individuals according to parents' status. Education once again became a means of upward social mobility, but intellectuals, researchers and technicians remained thin on the ground. Furthermore, their salary and quality of life scarcely differed from, and were sometimes inferior to, those of workers and employees. Pursuing an intellectual profession remained non-prestigious and still somewhat 'dubious'. Economic capital began to become a social resource, but to a limited extent. Many were hesitant to 'plunge into the sea' (*xiahai*) of capitalism, as the saying of the time had it. Firstly, profits were moderate. Secondly, development possibilities were circumscribed by low living standards and consumption. Finally, capitalism still had a whiff of heresy about it. Those who invested in capitalism placed themselves under the protection of government departments or belonged to the marginal strata of the population: unemployed youth; individuals who had been in trouble with the police, whether for political or criminal reasons; the disabled; educated youth sent to the countryside who were no longer able to pursue their studies. They were therefore activities that afforded little prestige, limited benefits, and still seemed dangerous to the great majority of the population. Money remained an ambiguous value.

The Time of Fractures (1992–2007)

While many questions have been raised about the meaning of the Tiananmen movement, few remain about its consequences. In 1992, it was no longer simply a question of a return to reforms, but of their acceleration and radicalisation. Hence-

THE TIANANMEN MOVEMENT

This subject would merit a volume in its own right and we still lack the historical distance to assess the phenomenon fully.[14] Let us nevertheless note that it was not a revolution by the popular classes seeking to overthrow a detested regime. Everyone, or nearly everyone, demonstrated in the Square, including prosecutors and police officers; and the movement had strong support at the highest levels of the leadership. The information available suggests that it represented a point of convergence of criticisms and questions about the country's present and future. China in the late 1980s was as if in 'suspension', its rulers not having decided between socialism and capitalism, or more precisely, trying to separate capitalist initiatives from the rest of the society. In doing so the Party preserved overall socialist order and social order but limited opportunities for a better life and upward social mobility. Daily life had improved considerably, but most people were demanding more. In the towns and cities—the movement was essentially urban—there was a profound sense of frustration about the closure of access routes to social mobility. Workers and employees in state enterprises, and their dependents, remained protected and privileged. But they noted that their income, eroded by inflation (which exceed 10 per cent in some years), was only increasing marginally. Their children became minor civil servants, employees or workers, or were 'waiting for' a job—a discreet term for unemployment. Individuals who had thrown themselves into the private economy found that their status did not match their contribution and the political risks they were running. Intellectuals had certainly lost their demeaning label, but their salaries remained low and their influence limited. Civil servants felt their position to be precarious because of the weakness of the legal system and the arbitrariness prevalent in the administrative system. Factory directors were trapped between the modesty of the reforms, which gave them few powers, and the competition of experts, who knew how to make the economy work. In government circles, debates occurred and doubts were expressed over the best way of accentuating and controlling change. In short, while the

43

Chinese had been summoned to the grand banquet of capital-ism, they could not yet partake in it.

The same confusion can be perceived in citizens' questions about the societal model that the country should follow. The 1980s were very rich intellectually. They witnessed the birth of a criti-cal Marxism and an indigenous liberalism, and a renaissance of philosophical currents that had disappeared years before. Ques-tions were asked about 'living together in the world',[15] the social use to which prosperity should be put, the type of society and political system that should be constructed, the mainsprings of social justice, the place and nature of democratic representation, and so forth. If freedom and democracy were perceived by all as crucial demands, the way they should be linked to Marxism, socialism, liberalism, etc. was still a matter of debate. The late 1980s were also a time of liberalisation. Certainly, 'rectification' movements periodically occurred, recalling that great suspicion of moral and political laissez-faire still existed among the lead-ership. Dissidents were arrested and deviants of all kinds expe-rienced serious problems. Nevertheless, it was possible to criticise the situation, to speak and form relationships with strangers, to travel inside and outside the country, and so on. At the beginning of 1989, as a very young PhD student the present author was able to visit prisons and juvenile delinquent rehabil-itation institutions with ease.

forth political debates focused exclusively on economic and social issues. The capitalist model of development popularised by the Asian Dragons (exploiting the labour of a poor, disci-plined and relatively educated population, attracting foreign capital and exporting at low prices) mixed with 'Chinese char-acteristics' became the ultimate horizon that would make Chi-nese people more satisfied and the country more powerful, while preserving order. If capital flowed in and exports grew, there would be more jobs and social mobility and hence less social protest. The most restless social strata—students, aca-demics, artists—would also find opportunities to derive greater advantages from the reformist policy. Made more competitive and open, public enterprises would be able to conquer new markets. Foreign investment and the enrichment of consumers would make China indispensable to the world. As for the out-sourcing of Taiwanese enterprises to the mainland, after a while it formed part of a strategy of reunification.[16]

Unlike many Western businessmen, we therefore cannot both celebrate China's growth and fret over the revival of nationalism. The entire history of nation-state building demonstrates that the political and the economic cannot be disconnected.[17] Capitalist accumulation in a territory, and improvements in the population's quality of life, assumes the construction of national identities. In the collective imaginary, individual prosperity, collective success and national self-assertion have to be seen as a single phenomenon, intended to ensure a position of strength abroad and social order at home. Modernisation, capitalism, and even democratisation are not, by themselves, factors of peaceful evolution.

It is striking to note that the radical policies of commodification of labour were accompanied by a concern for the 'social'. As if by reflex, the authorities almost immediately adopted measures aimed at the victims of reforms. This was the price to be paid for social protest not leading to political difficulties, even to a change of regime. But the timeliness with which social policies were adopted by the Chinese authorities at the end of the 1970s may be explained by two specific factors. The first is the social imaginary formed in the socialist era, obliging the authorities to combat poverty and destitution so as to avoid unrest. The second is the spontaneous reactions any society displays in order to protect social stability, a phenomenon Polanyi has analysed in detail.[18] The free market is always trying to emancipate itself from the social and political realities and then to impose its own rules. But the society responds by introducing policies of social protection.

45

At the outset, 'social policies' were disparate collections of partial measures. Those laid off from public enterprises were allowed to become the owners of their flats; a minimum income (*dibao*) was established for the urban population and, more recently, for a portion of rural dwellers; a special status and specific aid were created for those dismissed (*Xiagang zhigong*: literally, workers and employees removed from their posts). As in Europe decades ago,[19] they assumed the form of genuine social policies at the end of the 1990s and the beginning of the twenty-first century, with the development of a new system of social security that, while far from covering the whole population and all risks, made it possible to limit social exclusion.[20] The phenomenon of 'homelessness' is a marginal reality in China. Drug consumption has developed, but affects very small fringes of the population. Prostitution is monitored by the police and army. Crime—at all events, the kind that has the most impact on feelings of insecurity, rather than corruption—is negligible in comparison with Western countries.

Politically, debates grew poorer. Everyone seems to agree that market democracy must be China's ultimate horizon, but that it is first necessary to bolster this dynamic through prosperity and the assertion of national unity, to make China a wealthy, united nation, and to 'civilise' the lower classes. Among those who took part in the Tiananmen movement, and who had sometimes been active in 1979, some, but very few, aligned themselves with 'dissidence'. Most, including victims of the repression, were converted. They are artists, businessmen, academics. In this domain, the dynamic of assimilation of the elites has worked well. We might speak of a 'treason of the intellectuals', but also, more simply, of a new status for intellectuals, who participate in policy decisions. Many critical researchers are advisers to princes, who are increasingly attentive to their expertise.

It is right to get rich

Getting rich is now not merely tolerated, but justified. In Deng Xiaoping's famous formula, some people must 'get rich first' (*xian fuqilai*), before Chinese society as a whole can enjoy prosperity. It is legitimate to drive a Porsche or Ferrari, to live in a luxury flat, to spend on a meal what a peasant earns in several years' hard work, as long as it serves the long-term interests of the whole population. Economic capital has become an important element in social classification. More revealingly, businessmen are becoming politically important. Frequently at the junction of the public and the private, often the sons of cadres but graduates of foreign schools, they enter the Party and government bodies as representatives of the market economy. From this standpoint, the emergence in 2000–1 of the 'three represents' theory (*san ge daibiao*) is a key moment in the process. According to it, the Party must represent the interests of three forces: the people (the whole population), cultural circles, and the 'progressive productive forces' (that is, economic circles). In fact, success in business has become an official route to political influence.

Deindustrialisation: the fall of the public empire

Since the mid-1990s, the authorities have prioritised a policy geared to 'modernising' the public productive apparatus. The idea is to retain and regroup profitable assets and 'drop the rest'. The operation presupposes a complete overhaul of public employment and hence of the system of work units. Besides, the requisite consolidation of public enterprises, preliminary to their growth and entry onto the international stage, involves the disappearance of the dual burden of social protection and over-manning. The oldest and least skilled employees are dismissed, 'removed from their post' (*xiagang*—an arrangement

47

THE 'THREE REPRESENTS' AND THE PARTY

In sum, this new theory asserts the need to confer a power of representation via the Party on three social strata: the people, intellectuals, and—a novelty—business circles. The 'three represents' seems to be an attempt to justify the growing role of businessmen, major and minor, and of the upper middle classes from the standpoint of a 'popular' politics. More and more businessmen are appointed to the National People's Congress and the Chinese People's Political Consultative Conference, which are supposed to comprise the country's interest groups. During the last congress of the Communist Party (2012), the delegates included 160 multimillionaires. In 2011, directors and cadres of enterprises and members of the higher professions accounted for more than a quarter of Party members, although they only comprise a very small proportion of the population (see Chapter 3). More significant still, the Party has become younger. Around 80 per cent of new members are under 35; and this age group represented a quarter of the 80 million members in 2011. The same year, 40 per cent of new members were students. One of the Party's objectives is to improve the level of its membership.

under which they receive a paltry compensation from their employers) or are sent into early retirement, especially in the case of women. In total, between 50 and 60 million workers and employees lost their jobs between 1995 and the beginning of the 2000s.

The whole public economy has been hit by this swingeing reform. But industry, especially heavy industry, has paid the heaviest price. The major regions of the north and north-east have been completely de-industrialised, and are experiencing a social crisis whose social effects are ongoing. The class of workers and employees has been drastically diminished. Some have gone into early retirement (above all women, sometimes as young as 45), some survive on odd jobs, and others have been able to take advantage of specific local arrangements to find another job. Most have been able to maintain a certain standard of living thanks to the help of their child, the opportunity to keep their flat, and aid from local government. The restructuring of public employment has led to strong growth in non-state enterprises and hence a widening of income differentials. The administrative grid has been replaced by an infinite variety of working conditions and wages.[21]

Table 2: Public Employment in Urban Enterprises

Years	1996	2012
Employees in state-owned enterprises (millions)	112	60

Source: *China Statistical Yearbook 2009; National Bureau of statistics of China*

'Privatisation': a user's manual

There is much talk of the exponential growth of the private economy in China and the figures seem to confirm this. Many international organisations and journalists believe that employment in the private economy now greatly exceeds employment in the public sector. In reality, this assessment must be qualified. According to official data, the state is no longer an important employer in urban areas. In 2012, the number of employees in state-owned enterprises was only just over 60 million. However, something of a misuse of language is involved when reference is made to the private sector, because the 'non-public' sector combines highly disparate forms of ownership and owners (self-employed, private, foreign enterprises), the only common factor being that the companies are not state enterprises, that is to say controlled by Beijing. But whether directly, or via a succession of holdings, public bodies (municipalities, public bodies like trade unions, etc.) and public enterprises still have a significant stake in the capital of these non-public enterprises. Moreover, 'privatisation' has often involved a sleight of hand, with groups of civil servants picking up the most profitable parts of dismantled public enterprises. Secondly, let us also note that crucial sectors (energy, arms, raw materials, finance, transport) remain under the control of the major state companies. In 2012, of the 500 largest Chinese enterprises, 316 belonged to the state. Energy, transport, telecommunications, real estate and banks are under the control of these firms, which are now transnational. They are systematically favoured by the state. State enterprises only pay 2 per cent in tax on their profits and those that run into difficulties are generously bailed out by the public treasury. Finally, whatever the status of enterprises, it is difficult to disentangle politics from business. Doing business from the outset involves being integrated into networks that supply services in exchange for various benefits or simply political backing.[22]

POLITICS AND BUSINESS THROUGH THE REFORMS

Madame Liu is a businesswoman. She started in the 1980s with a small private restaurant, before branching out into different activities (trade and real estate, in the main). I questioned her about her relations with the authorities in the context of her business affairs.

'Things have changed a lot in this respect. In the 1980s, no one was interested in the private economy. Government departments created their own enterprises and civil servants earned a bit of money by "managing" these enterprises, which had a monopoly in important sectors. Opening a restaurant or shop was regarded as a bit dangerous, a bit "immoral". It only took a few notes to obtain authorisation and no one came to "extort" money from you. Then things became complicated. People saw that the private economy was becoming established, that it brought in money. And then everyone wanted to get in on the act. The police, the trade and industry departments, the hygiene office, etc. You really had the impression of being a "cash cow". And then the system became established. You now knew that in a district each policeman had his block, which he had to "manage". At a higher level—in my case, for example—I know it's necessary to give to so-and-so, so-and-so, etc. But once it's done, it's done. People don't come back.

Civil servants have an interest in not going too far. On the one hand, because they might give the impression that they are "dishonest", etc. You take precautions sometimes; you hand over the sum in front of witnesses. That's a way of putting pressure. On the other hand, everyone knows that civil servants and businessmen have got to prosper together: it's the role of civil servants to develop the economy. We're respected now. In places where the private economy is strong, employers can exert pressure on political decisions, but because we're useful to the career of politicians. No negotiations with employers, no business; no business, no growth; no growth, no promotion. We've got relations of mutual development. That's why to say that this is private, that is public, this is business, that is politics—none of it means much.'

(Interview conducted in October 2009).

In short, when it comes to employment, the public/private dichotomy is uninformative. What matters is not the formal ownership of an enterprise but the status of the individuals, families, enterprises or cliques who control it and the way it is managed. In a society in the throes of radical change, where the ambiguity of positions is a mainspring of economic growth, many individuals and interest groups straddle several categories. We can nevertheless conclude that if the public sector has declined significantly, to the benefit of operators of a more complex kind, it remains a significant element in urban employment and the economy generally, in particular via state enterprises monopolising the core sectors of the economy and the quasi monopoly of the state on the education system.

Development of the service sector

The Chinese economy has experienced a marked move towards the development of service sector employment, at the expense of the primary sector—a dynamic attributable to the development of certain economic areas (banking, commerce, advertising, media). New professions have emerged (specialists in human resources, sporting events organisers, breeders of domestic animals, artistic or legal professions), and personal services (cleaning ladies, carers for the elderly) have expanded significantly. In industry, posts for engineers and technicians represent a growing proportion of total employment. At the same time, individual entrepreneurs are substantially increasing their share in employment, as are the bosses of private enterprises and senior cadres in large enterprises.

Table 3: Distribution of GDP and Employment by Economic Sector in Percentage

Year	1978	2012
Primary		
(GDP)	28.2	10.1
(Employment)	71.0	33.6
Secondary		
(GDP)	47.9	45.3
(Employment)	17.0	30.3
Tertiary		
(GDP)	23.9	44.6
(Employment)	12.0	36.1

Sources: China Statistical Yearbook 2012 and National Bureau of Statistics of China

New industrialisation

The socialist working class has been replaced by one born of rural migration. It is divided into several categories. Firstly, peasants migrating to the development zones of the south—in particular, the provinces of Guangdong and Fujian—and most of the large towns and cities. Secondly, construction workers—this sector almost exclusively employs rural immigrants. And finally, the urban services sector (small shops, rubbish collection, cleaning, domestic servants, garden maintenance, etc.). The very harsh living and working conditions people experience do not prevent them from often having a very positive view of their situation. Migration is as much motivated by the quest for improved living standards—which can easily be five or even ten times better—as by opportunities for a new experience: that of urban modernity. Consequently, many of the 236 million migrants (2012 figures) do not envisage returning home—a change of orientation that Chinese researchers and leaders have now largely integrated into their analyses and policies. The task ahead is one of compelling local authorities to find concrete solutions for this mammoth reorganisation of urban society.

Table 4: Distribution of Total Employment

Year	1978	2008
Total employment (millions)	401	767
Urban employment (millions)	95	371
Rural employment (millions)	306	396

Source: China Statistical Yearbook 2009

Education as a decisive asset

Since the start of the 1990s the authorities have been investing massively in education. However, this effort is characterised by two major imbalances. On the one hand, it predominantly involves secondary schools and higher education institutions, which have seen their numbers expand very significantly. On the other hand, it essentially benefits the urban population. For a few years now, local authorities have been responsible for a large proportion of education expenditure, which places them in situations of very marked inequality. Primary and secondary schools and colleges in the Chinese countryside are infinitely less well-equipped than urban ones. The quality of teachers there is low and, in general, they are less well-informed on the examination subjects than their urban colleagues. As at each grade there is competition between pupils to get into good schools and good classes, it is necessary to pay for after-school tuition, something poor families cannot afford.

Furthermore, selection mechanisms limit peasant access to universities. The inhabitants of developed provinces have less need of good marks in university entrance exams than those from remote provinces, and this is even truer for the most prestigious universities (see Chapter 3).

Very often, the children of migrants cannot do the courses at urban state schools, either because they are rejected, or because high supplementary fees are demanded. They must then make do with establishments on the margins of legality, created by migrants, which are worse than mediocre. The children of migrants do not have the right to take university entry exams in their actual place of residence and therefore cannot benefit from the advantages enjoyed by their urban peers. Logically enough, such *de facto* or *de jure* forms of discrimination lead to inequalities in access to university. In an as yet unpublished study of students at Tsinghua University that I supervised in 2010, it was observed that 72.4 per cent of students were urban, whereas the percentage of urban residents in the whole population was only 45.7 per cent. More striking still, cultural capital was indispensable for success: 55.6 per cent of students had fathers who were university graduates, whereas the percentage of university graduates in the total male population was only 6 per cent. Finally, while 29 per cent of students came from families whose head had a profession that placed him among the elites, the latter only represented 6 per cent of the total population.

A sharp increase in the number of university places at the beginning of the 2000s did not reduce inequalities. From 1999 to 2004 the number of university places increased by 20 per cent every year. Nevertheless, the new students were mainly from urban families belonging to the lower middle classes while many children from the upper middle classes took advantage of the opportunity to enter the best universities.

The promotion of education has been accompanied by an increase in education levels in every profession. Whereas it was enough to have completed secondary school ten or fifteen years ago, it is now necessary to have a bachelor's or master's degree. Even so, not everything is rosy in the country of the super-qualified. Graduate unemployment has emerged in recent years. Here too, however, there is marked discrimination. Those who encounter the greatest difficulties are the graduates of second-class universities, who therefore 'only just' got into university. These lucky ones, who have profited from the democratisation of higher education, generally hail from the lower strata, the countryside or small towns, and do not possess the social capital required to find a good job.

Urbanisation

Growth has been accompanied by a notable increase in the population of cities and an expansion of urban areas. In 2012, the rate of urbanisation reached 52.57 per cent of the total

THE BIRTH OF UNEMPLOYMENT:
AT THE BOTTOM AND TOP OF THE SCALE

Officially, unemployment is very low—4.1 per cent of the working population in 2012. However, this figure only applies to the urban population. Many rural labourers periodically find themselves without work. This was massively the case in 2008–9, when the financial crisis immediately led to the dismissal of 20 million workers without any alteration in the unemployment rate. Official unemployment does not encompass people who have never been employed, those placed in early retirement and who would like to work, those who have resigned, those who have failed to register, and so on. In the main, only employees who have been dismissed prior to the termination of their contract are counted. According to a 2012 survey, the unemployment rate would have been 8.05 per cent if migrant workers were included.[23] It seems that elderly migrants are the main victims of unemployment.

Yet Chinese society is grappling with a chronic crisis of employment. It is partially concealed by low levels of pay: it is not very expensive to add a few posts. Everywhere, including on construction sites or in textile factories, over-manning is rife. Even if workers put in long hours, the often rudimentary work organisation and equipment reduce labour productivity significantly. In the tertiary sector, labour is just as abundant, in offices and shops and restaurants alike. The authorities put pressure on investors to employ the maximum number of locals, particularly youth. Despite this, urban youths without a degree find it difficult to get hired. They often do temporary jobs on work placements before finding badly paid regular work, often thanks to their social capital.

More seriously, while students from the major universities and highly-valued specialists (hard sciences and engineering science, law, business, etc.) have no difficulty finding work at a reasonable salary—albeit less easily and at an inferior level than a few years back—the same is not true of the bulk of the cohort. The press regularly reports cases of suicide by desperate young graduates.

Certainly, graduates are more demanding and all of them want to work in the big towns and cities, which guarantees better career prospects and a more exciting life. Rather than accept any offer whatsoever, they prefer to remain the responsibility of their parents for a time. We might note that here too, the quality of the network of relations is a key element in entering the world of work. String pulling is often as important a tool as a degree.

Even so, the significant increase in the number of graduates and the low quality of jobs created for each per cent of growth lead to a certain saturation of the graduate market. In 2013, Beijing universities graduated 229,000 students but only 98 000 jobs were available.[24] In April 2013, a survey revealed that only 35 per cent of those about to graduate had secured employment.[25] The average salary on being hired is declining regularly and it is not uncommon to find business school graduates who speak one or two foreign languages starting at 3,000 yuan a month, a salary equivalent to that of many migrants. According to a survey realised by Tsinghua University, in 2011 the average level of the first job for graduates was 2,719 yuan, and 69 per cent of them receive less than 2,000 yuan. The same year, the average wage of migrant workers reached 2,049 yuan. Certainly, graduates have far better working conditions than migrant workers, and once having accumulated experience they see their wage increasing very rapidly. But many students are disappointed by what they find in the labour market compared to what they expected.[26]

population and urban employment accounts for 48.4 per cent of total employment. Urban growth obviously affects the big towns and cities, but also the medium-sized towns, which absorb ever more migrants of rural origin. Under the rubric of 'migration', we must distinguish between two movements. The first—a minority one—concerns skilled, or even highly-skilled, labour, which accompanies the growth of the major economic zones. For example, students from other towns remain in Shanghai or Beijing after obtaining their degree. The second movement affects the bulk of migration, involving enormous battalions of peasant labourers (*nongmingong*).

In both cases, urban integration comes up against the maintenance of the statutory dualism based on residence, but with different consequences. 'Temporary resident' identity does not confer access to public services (education, social security, social housing, continuing education, etc.), even if some improvements are to be noted in this respect. But for skilled labour, there is minimum inconvenience: their income is often sufficient to enable them to get around it. Nothing of the sort applies to the 'new working class'.

Furthermore, the situation varies with the size of the town. In the major conurbations, the system remains rigid and even the purchase of a flat is no longer a guarantee of urban integration. By contrast, in the medium-sized towns the process is largely in train: the *hukou* can be obtained readily enough.[27] The gap between migrant and indigenous populations is low there and homogenisation therefore presents fewer problems.

Urbanisation must also be considered from the standpoint of the social imaginary. The negative image of the city projected by the regime until the 1980s has been replaced by the image of an urban space identified with progress. The city is no longer the symbol of debauchery, inequality, injustice, or economic and behavioural immorality. On the contrary, it is the site of modernity, culture, education, civility, and opportunities for personal fulfilment. It is where one becomes a modern Chinese and thus, in a way, a person 'of quality'. The integration of the population of rural origin is therefore also a cultural issue.

The break-up of the social security systems

The disappearance of the work unit system has left a big vacuum, which the authorities have found difficult to fill. A system of protection now exists, covering accidents at work, retirement, illness and maternity risks, and unemployment. But it does not cover the whole working population in the towns and covers very few individuals in rural areas. In fact, several conditions have to be met to be included in these insurance provisions, whose funds derive from employers and employees: possession of a work contract, having an employer who pays contributions, and, essentially, being an urban resident. Another major problem is that contributions are far from covering expenditure. The size of the informal economy and the reluctance of employers reduces the available funds, while the ageing of the population, on the one hand, and the considerable increase in medical costs, on the other, make it increasingly difficult to meet the expenses of those insured.

Let us try to clarify things. Almost all town-dwellers are covered on condition that they have a work contract. Even when workers have medical cover, it only involves a proportion of medical costs. In the case of an operation or serious illness, patients have to meet much of the bill, sell goods, or borrow sizeable sums from friends or family. The end of the work unit has been accompanied by a privatisation of healthcare. Hospitals remain public, but are managed as private enterprises and with a total lack of transparency. Patients have to accept pointless supplementary treatments, doctors demand bribes, and medicines are over-manufactured. Certainly, this money partially serves the modernisation of hospitals, but such malfeasance contributes to a continuous increase in health expenses and a growth in the share for which patients are responsible. Getting treated has become a source of anxiety for the Chinese population.

Among wage-earners too, inequalities are pronounced. Civil servants benefit from the best social protection.[28] White-collar staff in large enterprises often enjoy advantageous social packages, comprising additional or private insurance. As the size of enterprises diminishes, and we leave the big towns and cities, the situation deteriorates. Moreover, social security funds are municipalised: benefits depend wholly on the sums collected *in situ*. Towns in difficulty have small resources for a multiplicity of needs; the reverse is true of prosperous municipalities. Weak equalising mechanisms have been established on an experimental basis at a provincial level, but no large-scale reform has emerged, even if centralisation increasingly seems to be an objective.

HOUSING: OWNERSHIP AND SEGREGATION

With housing no longer being supplied by the employer, access to this good likewise generates social divisions. The urban poor are housed without difficulty, either because they are owners of a flat passed on to them by their former employer, or because they benefit from social assistance. Migrants must find their own housing or rely on their employer (construction sector). If of a certain age, the average urban resident has been able to purchase the flat he occupied cheaply and possibly buy another. Individual entrepreneurs and small employers must rent or buy their housing at market prices. As for civil servants, their access to property is subsidised by the state.

The problem facing the young is different. They have not obtained a flat through their work unit and must borrow from banks or their family. Indebtedness is sometimes heavy and debtors become what the press call 'property slaves', devoting a significant proportion of their income to this budgetary item. More than 91 per cent of flat purchases are made by mortgage. Among such borrowers, more than a third reimburse a sum greater than 50 per cent of their salary.[29]

The absence of a social housing sector is one of the problems confronted by the urban population. No provision is made for migrants, who will soon no longer be able to house themselves as a result of the disappearance of the old accommodation. Moreover, the state does not really have a policy of countering spatial segregation. Land speculation is expelling lower strata to suburban zones that are increasingly distant from the centre.

As for migrants and peasants, they only enjoy a very low level of social security. In the case of migrants, we note the existence of various local measures. For peasants, the only serious initiative is the creation of a mutual fund (*xinnonghe*) financed by those insured (20 yuan a year), the central government and local authorities, which is intended to reimburse medical costs. The whole rural population was due to be included in 2009. However, the further the hospital lies from the place of residence—in other words, the more serious the illness and the higher the medical costs—the greater is the share for which the insured are responsible.

The regression in protection has given rise to a form of hitherto unknown urban poverty. Those affected never fall into absolute poverty because of the existence of a minimum income (*dibao*) and one-off forms of assistance for health problems. But the sums allocated are very small and the recipients do not have access to the best medical treatment.

3

A NEW SOCIETY

Since the late 1990s, Chinese society has been engaged in a great debate on social stratification. What criteria should determine social status? What form should society take, in terms of social strata, and the relative size of each of them, in order to achieve the highest level of political stability and economic growth? The responses are pretty much consistent with modernisation theory: it is a question of hitting upon the ideal rational formula. Nevertheless, the search for a norm cannot avert conflicts emerging between social categories or prevent such 'class struggle' endangering the fragile consensus over the dual imperative of prosperity and social order.

The emergence of this debate and these conflicts is bound up with the scale and speed of the upheavals experienced by China since the 1990s. These abrupt changes find an echo in many and various forms of deviance, anxiety about the increased competition between individuals, frustration due to the opening up of possibilities and the proliferation of social movements. Consequently, rulers and experts have been prompted to reflect on mechanisms for managing society rather than dominating or even controlling it. Conversely, the 'social'—a new sphere in which there is no distinction between the private and the public, in which everything is perceived in terms of household problems: production, income, consumption, etc.—pervades the concerns of politicians. But such questions are not merely technical; they also refer to major issues of ideology and the imaginary. While the Communist Party remains in power, the new social situation is forcing it to come up with a new discourse without calling socialist principles into question. The Party and its servants remain 'at the service of the people' and the great project of modernising the nation. Leaders formed in the school of socialism cannot disavow their views without imperilling their identity and historical legitimacy. A kind of ideological inertia obtains, whose source lies in the still living memory of the experiences of rulers and population prior to the reforms. As for the younger generations, they are certainly growing up in a new world, but it is shaped by previous generations (parents, teachers, officials in enterprises or government departments).

The Conditions of Social Mobility

In terms of social mobility, there have been major changes. Intellectuals and artists have gone from pariah status to a seat at the top table. The bosses of private enterprises are well established. Many peasants have abandoned the land and very significantly improved their quality of life. Some categories have disappeared; others have emerged. However, by way of social origin and networks of relations, the structures of socialist society continue to determine individual trajectories powerfully. The difference from the preceding period stems from a diversification in the resources that facilitate social success, as well as a multiplication of opportunities for combining these resources. New fields of accumulation of goods and power have been opened up to ambitious, skilful outsiders, but their ability to climb still has its limits.

Determinants

Place of birth and of residence still, in part, determines the fate of individuals. The importance now attributed to education has given urban residents, who control access to it, an undoubted advantage. Urban status also imparts prestige and, consequently, a certain assertiveness to those who enjoy it. Belonging to the urban universe also supplies an effective social network. By contrast, the rural space condemns people to a negative identity in terms not only of cultural capital, but also of symbolic capital and hence self-confidence. When talking about possibilities of upward social mobility through study, professional training or 'urbanising' their behaviour many rural residents take the attitude that it is not for them. Migration causes peasants to lose the social and political capital they started out with, while maintenance of the residence system and the social segregation they suffer at the hands of the indigenous population presents an often crippling obstacle to their integration into cities.[1]

Political and relational resources retain their importance, but they are more closely connected with other forms of capital.[2] To get a good job, it is necessary to resort to string-pulling but also to have a degree. Party membership remains important but its influence has become blurred. Massive recruitment among the new social strata (in particular, employers and white-collar staff), and the co-option this entails, make it difficult to evaluate the role of membership. In the constant flow of social competition, where forms of capital are constantly interacting, it is difficult to assess the role of a particular resource. We do not know whether an employer's business is flourishing thanks to his inscription in the Party, or whether his inscription in the Party is a result of his success in business. More precisely, it is possible to cite cases that tend one way or the other, but not to assess the phenomenon for society as a whole. At all events, it can be said that there is a symbiosis of economic success and political capital. As for social capital, it functions in the same way. A good social level is a measure of success, but social success (getting rich, a good job, a good education) improves this level.

Educational qualifications are now indispensable, especially for the younger generation (members of the older generation can maintain their positions and prestige thanks to their political and social resources). Being born into an influential family, with wide relational ramifications, is a powerful advantage, but it must be complemented by a university degree, foreign experience and the adoption of a style that accords with civilised, progressive values.[3]

The big winner of the period seems to be economic capital, whether in the form of income or property. Becoming rich brings political and social power, as well as, obviously, prestige. However, while money and conspicuous consumption have unquestionably become determining elements in classification, the wealthy do not escape criticism. The concentration of wealth in the hands of a few and the 'nouveau riche' style of multi-millionaires provoke violent criticisms, in popular and official discourse alike.

The type of employer also plays a not insignificant role in social classification—in particular, in terms of access to social security provisions and social advantages. To be employed in a large enterprise, whether Chinese or foreign, or a government department often guarantees a significant level of social benefits. Conversely, individual entrepreneurs and even restaurant employees must meet their health, education and housing expenses themselves.

PERSONAL MERIT AND SOCIAL DETERMINATION: WHAT IS AT STAKE IN THE *GAOKAO*

Since the 1980s, the national competitive exam for recruitment to university (*gaokao*) has been one of the main vectors of personal success. Those without a university degree will experience great difficulty finding a good job. Conversely, students from one of the top universities like Tsinghua (Beijing), Beijing University or Fudan (Shanghai) have a key that will open many doors. Obviously, some can employ other means to obtain a place in the sun, but this is out of most people's reach and even the powerful now need to exploit the surplus symbolic capital provided by a degree.

The examination occurs once a year in June and lasts nine hours, spread over three days. The number of candidates was 9.15 million in 2012 as against 1.64 million in 1984 and over this period the pass rate has increased from 29 per cent to 75 per cent. It has already been mentioned in Chapter 2 that the number of students enrolled in higher education dramatically increased at the beginning of the 2000s. This trend has continued: in 2012, 27 per cent of the age cohort was enrolled as against 6 per cent in 2005. For most candidates, what is most at stake is obtaining enough marks to enter a first-rank university, each university having a precise ranking in the official ratings.

As a consequence of the democratisation of education, the number of students in higher education increases regularly. In 2011, China had 2,762 higher education establishments, a two-fold increase in ten years. According to the National Bureau of Statistics of China, the total number of students was 23.9 million in 2012 as against 17.33 million in 2005. There were 5.4 million new enrolments in 2005 and 6.9 million in 2012. Between these dates the number of students graduating increased from 3.77 to 6.24 million, rising to 6.9 million in 2013. There were about 340,000 Chinese students in foreign universities in 2011 (14 per cent of the total of foreign students in world universities).

The *gaokao* does not claim to be meritocratic. There is no comparison with systems where everyone is supposed to start on the same footing despite the social standing of their parents, hypocritical as they are. The number of marks obtained in the exam determines access to university according to one's place of residence. For example, a pupil from Guangxi needs more marks than a pupil from Beijing to access higher education, and many more if he wants to enter a Beijing university. In other words, places are reserved for the most developed provinces and towns and cities. More than 80 per cent of pupils from Beijing who take the *gaokao* pass it and most of them enter the best universities. Above all, places are reserved in universities for natives of that area. Thus, every year, people from Beijing enjoy special quotas in the city's universities; the same applies to Shanghai (and the best universities are to be found in the major cities on the coast). In recent years, an inhabitant of Xinjiang has no chance of doing social sciences at Tsinghua, because no places are provided in this specialism for these provinces. More than 50 per cent of students from Beijing who pass the competition go to a Beijing university and 20 per cent enter a top rank university (whatever its location).

Every candidate must choose three or four universities and a number of subjects that he or she wishes to study. They will get their options depending on their results. They also have to choose between a 'humanities' and a 'sciences' path and three optional subjects. Mathematics, Chinese and English are obligatory. More than 90 per cent of students who achieve the best scores opt for Tsinghua or Beida in Beijing, or Fudan in Shanghai. In 2008, only 0.03 per cent of candidates succeeded in getting into one of the first two. The value of their degrees can be imagined.

Outside this competitive exam, it is possible to get to university via two very narrow routes. A few dozen places are reserved for exceptional pupils (such as athletes and the 'exceptionally gifted'); and quotas are sometimes negotiated by mutual agreement between universities and some secondary schools. It is here that corruption or string-pulling can come into play.

The *gaokao* is a terrible source of anxiety. Most candidates spend their last year at school working 13 or 14 hours a day without a break. For three days, China (especially urban China) holds its breath. Most parents pamper their only child for years on end so that they can continue the family's social ascent. Having spent enormous sums on additional courses and the purchase of educational materials, they ruin themselves making offerings in Buddhist temples. Some are ready to pay bribes, or organise rigging, for their offspring to succeed. Every year, scandals break out.

Let us specify that the exam is based on multiple choice questions and puts the onus on memory. Most criticisms focus on this aspect of the competition. Students are not prepared for analysis or personal reflection. Furthermore, this selective system immediately excludes brilliant students who possess different forms of intelligence from those promoted by the *gaokao*.

The opening up of possibilities

Nevertheless, the determination of fates is less definitive than it used to be. As we have seen, many social categories are ambiguous—their members are neither truly urban, nor truly rural, neither employed nor unemployed, or at a stage of upward social mobility without guarantees for the future. The converse of the growing insecurity of statuses is that there are greater possibilities for social mobility than in the past. For a start, geographical mobility has introduced a galvanising effect, whose impact is not altogether cancelled by the maintenance of the residence system. The norms of the 'just and unjust' are undergoing rapid change in the countryside.[4] Depending on the situation, in conflicts people can rely on norms derived from custom, socialist principles, or more recent legal provisions. At the level of argument and action alike, people are equipped with various weapons.

The policy of integrating migrants slowly but allowing them to come to the cities almost at will provides opportunities for creating new relational networks. Investigations indicate that

69

migrants increasingly mix with city-dwellers and sometimes create fairly close relations with them. Certainly, these are often relations of exploitation or, at best, of paternalism between a relatively privileged population and a culturally and economically inferior group. But many districts have 'their' migrants, whose dynamism they make use of while protecting them from the police or tax authorities. Such migrants sometimes make the most of the situation, become small employers, and manage to place their offspring in a good urban school. Vast numbers of migrants are excluded from these forms of cohabitation, particularly in the construction sector or manufacturing industry, where labourers are housed on-site. But they are central to questions of urbanisation. Greater integration of migrants presupposes a certain form of social diversity.

Like urban residents, many migrants look to the future. Their objective is to settle in the city in order to pursue a more or less specific project of social ascent. Others think about returning to the countryside to start up an enterprise. But these are not mutually exclusive options. During an investigation in Shanxi, I met numerous migrants who had opened a shop or created a small business in their village, while continuing to do business in the city. In other words, choices are no longer necessarily restricted to a zero-sum game. On the contrary, cities—their networks, opportunities and demand—can be combined with the advantages possessed by the migrant in his or her region of origin.

A further element of mobility consists in the diversification of professions. Migrants occupy niches (small shops, waiting, street cleaning) connected with economic growth and urbanisation. The sons or daughters of workers or employees have profited from the urban quasi-monopoly over education to obtain what are sometimes highly skilled jobs.

Finally, money itself galvanises the social hierarchy. Through corruption or the sharing of the fruits of business, it is possible to transform recently acquired economic capital into political and social capital. A perverse effect, perhaps, but one that enables some people to escape their condition and which imparts greater fluidity to power relations.

The Morphology of Chinese Society

Most attempts to classify Chinese society use profession, economic resources, education and networks of relations as distinguishing criteria. Here we find a Weberian influence at odds with the Marxist dogma that was predominant until the mid-1990s. Only then did people begin to refer to prestige, education and so forth as factors of social identity and stratification and, at the same time, to the middle class. In fact, the latter plays the role of 'reference class' in assessing current stratification and the adjustments it needs to undergo.

In this set of criteria, profession plays the principal role in attempts to synthesise social stratification. Because of the scale of informal income and undeclared work, economic resources are an insufficiently precise factor. As for education, the fact that its role is relatively recent, and only involves young generations on a mass scale, renders it of limited use. The authoritative classification was established by Lu Xueyi and researchers from the Chinese Academy of Social Sciences on the basis of socio-professional categories. It is based on the existence of ten groups, often combined by researchers into three social strata. The upper strata (leaders, managers, owners of private enterprises) accumulate the main decisive resources (economic, political, educational, social) in significant quantities, directly or via exchange. The middle strata (individual entrepreneurs, technicians, administrative staff) possess some resources (educational or economic) in large quantities and others in very low quantities. Their political and social capital is significantly inferior to the upper strata. Finally, the lower strata possess resources in extremely limited quantities.

CHINESE SOCIAL STRATIFICATION: A SOCIO-PROFESSIONAL CATEGORISATION

Lu Xueyi and researchers from the Chinese Academy of Social Sciences have classified Chinese society on the basis of ten socio-professional categories:[5]

1. **Managers of social and state organisations** (*guojia yu shehui guanlizhe*) comprise the leaders of government and Party bodies, as well as those of social organisations (e.g. trade unions). They represent the upper stratum in nearly all spheres. They have extensive power and wide networks and their modest salary is amply supplemented by bonuses, benefits in kind and, finally, illegal or 'grey' income (dabbling on the stock market, a side business run by a family member, etc.). While 'technicians' have been able to break into this milieu, downward mobility is rare: 'many enter, few exit' (*duojin shaochu*).

2. **Owners of private enterprises** (*siying qiyezhu*) hail from all social milieus including rural dwellers. In reality, however, information about them is rather sketchy. They enjoy very high income and more and more political influence. Most of them are Party members and/or have official positions in local and national assemblies.

3. **Management staff** (*jingli renyuan*) refers to those in charge of enterprises or public bodies, who are, respectively, neither owners nor leaders. Recruitment is virtually the same as in the case of the previous category, but is more open.

4. **Professional and technical staff** (*zhuanye jishu renyuan*) comprise the staff of state and Party bodies and enterprises engaged in tasks requiring scientific and technical skills or a particular specialisation. For Chinese researchers, they represent the most stable and representative group of the middle class.

5. **Administrative staff** (*banshi renyuan*) constitute the stratum of lower 'white-collar' employees and their characteristics align them closely with the previous category. Such white-collar employees occupy the same posts as technicians, but in a subaltern position. This is a 'buffer' category containing the children of workers and employees, but also the children of higher strata who have failed in their studies.

6. **Individual commercial and industrial business owners** (*geti gongshanghu*) work alone or with their family and employ few or no personnel. They are artisans, shopkeepers, middlemen, and so forth. The level of social reproduction in this category is high and they have little chance of upward social mobility.

7. **Starting with trade and service sector employees** (*shangye yu fuwuye congyerenyuan*), we come to the lower strata of society.

8. **The stratum of industrial workers** (*chanye gongren*) is very disparate, since it contains the old urban workers, who are diminishing in numbers, and the migrant labourers who constitute the vast majority of this new working class.

9. **Farm workers** (*nongye laodongzhe*) evince very high rates of reproduction.

10. **Workless, unemployed, partially employed** (*wuye shiye banshiye renyuan*) comprise all categories of the unemployed, including those working on a casual basis.

The relations between these groups are characterised by:

1. An increasingly wide gap between them. The evolution of the Gini coefficient reveals a continual increase in income differentials between the richest and poorest. According to estimates, it ranges from 40 to 60 for recent years (compared with 30 in the 1980s)—far in excess of Scandinavian countries (24 to 26) or Western Europe (32 to 34); higher than the United States

(40.8); and only lower than most African and Latin American counties (45 to 58).[6] According to an investigation carried out in 2011, the 10 per cent richest Chinese own 57 per cent of income and 85 per cent of the country's wealth. In brief, resources are increasingly concentrated in the same hands.

In the interviews I conducted with heads of firms during fieldwork in the 2000s, they expressed great satisfaction. They scarcely referred to the political obstacles confronting them any more. Some wanted the last rigidities in the labour market (the residence system) to go, but not all. The need for social stability was a given, which they had integrated into their analysis and strategy. Nearly all of them declared themselves highly satisfied with government policy and, in particular, the growing influence they had on public decisions. Their political integration, when not accomplished straight away (the case with the sons of cadres), seemed to be coming along nicely.

As for leaders and managers, their political positions and networks enable them to engage in business without any difficulty. Finally, the access of the upper strata to educational capital—particularly foreign degrees—is guaranteed. The mutual assimilation of the elites seems to be a reality.

2. Increasing difficulty in moving from one social group to another. Mobility between categories within a group is relatively easy, but there is a threshold effect between each of the ensembles. The obstacles to the entry process vary. The middle classes lack political and social capital—resources that can only be readily obtained through education or merit. As for the lower classes, they lack resources in all areas. It is for migrants that entry into the middle classes is most complex. In effect, a legal barrier exists which, although diminished, makes upward social mobility difficult. Furthermore, even in the absence of systemic obstacles, the social discrimination from which migrants suffer handicaps them in the race for success. Among the 'deprived', the urban unemployed emerge as privileged

because they enjoy a social safety net and a certain symbolic capital. This is not the case with the 'poor' of rural origin.[7]

Nevertheless, the low mobility between groups is balanced by broad possibilities for mobility within groups. Virtually any peasant can become a worker; nearly any member of the administrative staff can become a technician; and so forth. In this way, they can improve their income and social status. It should also be noted that in all professional sectors, it is people of the same generation—born between the 1940s and the 1950s—who occupy the dominant positions. The old principle of seniority is far from having disappeared.

Table 5: Weight of the Different Socio-Professional Categories in the Working Population (2006)

Occupation	Percentage of the population
Managers of state and social organizations (*guojia yu shehui guanlizhe*)	2.3%
Owners of private enterprises (*siying qiyezhu*)	1.3%
Management staff (*jingli renyuan*)	2.6%
Professional and technical staff (*zhuanye jishu renyuan*)	6.3%
Administrative staff (*banshi renyuan*)	7%
Individual commercial and industrial business owners (*geti gongshanghu*)	9.5%
Trade and service sector employees (*shangye yu fuwuye congyerenyuan*)	10.2%
Industrial workers (*chanye gongren*)	14.7%
Farm workers (*nongye laodongzhe*)	40.3%
Workless, unemployed, partially employed (*wuye shiye banshiye renyuan*)	5.9%

Source: Lu Xueyi (ed.), *Dangdai zhongguo shehui jiegou* [The Social Structure in China Today], Beijing: Shehui kexue wenxian, 2010

The Dangers of Imbalances

Everyone, be they researcher, civil servant, journalist or man in the street, is agreed that the pyramidal structure of the population (see Table 5) threatens serious imbalances in the short and medium terms. The upper classes (the first three categories) represent a narrow fringe, just 6.2 per cent, while the popular classes (the last four categories) make up 71.1 per cent and the middle classes only form a small group. Lu and other sociologists believe that the last group is constantly increasing—Lu speaks of an average growth of 1 per cent a year in its share of the total population—but most are concerned about this pyramid shape. For them, it contrasts with the model—posited as ideal—of Western societies, where stratification exhibits a spherical curve opposing two narrow poles (the rich and the poor) to an imposing mass of intermediate strata. The prominent sociologist Zhou Xiaohong concluded that the Chinese middle class is far from having emerged yet.[8]

Social frustrations

Widening gaps in condition create frustration among the lower strata. The press regularly reports the murder of bosses or the suicides of employees because of non-payment of wages. Migrants, who often receive a significant slice of their annual pay just before the Spring holiday, are especially affected by this on account of their often unclear contractual status and lack of legal protection. Desperate at not being able to take their pay packet back to the countryside, they sometimes commit suicide or resort to extreme measures. Gratuitous attacks on 'nobs' (*dakuan*) are also multiplying, particularly by victims of expropriation, in cities and country alike.

Some migrants fall into crime. According to more or less official statistics, 70–80 per cent of criminals are migrants. Such statistics are, certainly in part, an ideological effect of social inequalities. We know that the illegal acts most likely to be punished are those committed by members of the lower classes. Not only because they are often more visible, more violent, and less intelligently concealed (theft, homicide, etc.) than those committed by others (malfeasance, corruption, etc.), but also because their authors are more systematically arrested and sentenced. Finally, it is easy for the police to accuse an innocent migrant of a crime they have failed to resolve.

Similarly, the link between 'social problems' and crime is rather too mechanical. Sometimes popular milieus are more attached to norms than the upper strata. Nevertheless, it cannot be denied that the criminalisation of a section of migrants, particularly the new generation, is one consequence of their problems in integrating. Furthermore, the increasing and, above all, more conspicuous gap between the upper strata and the rest creates undeniable feelings of jealousy and injustice among disadvantaged groups. Such resentment of the 'heartless rich' (*weifu buren*) can produce hatred of the wealthy (*jiufu xinli*) when an event occurs to crystallise it. Party or government cadres have been assassinated simply because they were thought to be wealthy. Conversely, the upper strata live with a strong sense of insecurity. Without a doubt, wealth is more discreet in mainland China than Hong Kong and the legitimacy of ostentation has not been fully established.

The upper strata and the state are criticised, more or less explicitly in the work of researchers, and much more violently in popular discourse, for the way an unjust tax system, scheming and corruption prevent the popular classes from joining the middle class and some of the latter from acceding to leadership positions.

The population's frustrations are also expressed in proliferating social conflicts. Strikes and protest movements by migrants against their poor working, living and wage conditions; resistance to expropriation by juicy real estate operations whose cost they bear; the unrest of homeowners reacting against the malfeasance of 'developers' and residence management companies—all these demonstrate the existence of profound, collective discontent with the rules of the game.

A consumer society that consumes little

The goods on display in the street and significant rises in living standards are leading to a notable increase in consumption. However, despite appearances, the Chinese only consume a very small part of their income. The motor of the miracle still consists in the capacity of the Chinese economy to profit from global demand by attracting foreign capital, and not in domestic demand, whose weakness is a matter of concern to political circles and analysts. The Chinese consume little—36 per cent of GDP, or half the U.S. rate. But this propensity to save is not attributable to some cultural given. It is based on a sense of insecurity largely bound up with the low level of social security and public expenditure in certain areas.

Many Chinese have to compensate for the erosion of social protection. Even those who have cover know that it is minimal, particularly when it comes to health expenses. Those with a work contract, and their employers, make contributions towards a pension. But the relevant sums are low and the pension funds are regularly hit by scandals, creating doubt among the beneficiaries about the real possibilities of cover. Finally, the cost of educating the one permitted child is increasing dramatically. The cost of schooling, but also expenditure for additional courses, additional activities (sport or music), and even study or stays abroad, are putting a strain on the family budget. In this context, buying a flat or making significant savings represents a guarantee for old and new generations alike. Moreover, the rise in property prices and very low returns on savings compel everyone to put significant sums aside or to get into such debt that any form of consumption is considerably limited.

In this context, we can understand the importance assumed by the enjoyment of certain advantages like additional sickness insurance or old-age insurance, partial responsibility for a flat purchase, or occupation of a dwelling free of charge or at low cost (company or official accommodation). We can also understand why economists are concerned about the future. Voices stressing the need to propel growth by domestic demand, not foreign demand, have become ever more numerous since the Asian crisis of 1997 as world economic crises multiply. The issue of consumption has therefore become a major one. To climb higher and accumulate, the Chinese economy needs numerous, demanding consumers. For example, the multiplication of official holiday periods in the last few years is very clearly aimed at enabling the Chinese to travel and spend.

The Ideal Class

There is a complete consensus among Chinese people about this point: the absence of a middle class is preventing the 'smooth take-off' of a society that has been completely transformed by the reforms. Social stratification should take the shape of a rugby ball or olive. The ideal class, the middle class is perceived and presents itself, particularly in the press, as the one to ensure China's transition to modernity. It is supposed to ensure dynamism, rationality and stability. This is a slightly hasty and caricatural assessment. But it summarises the essence of current debates on the ideal stratification well enough. Such a caricature is to be taken all the more seriously in that it derives from the media, whether academic or mass public, a sector that is by definition controlled by the middle classes. Those who work in it, like those who read it, are middle class. We are therefore dealing with an interesting case of the mirror effect: the middle classes create a positive image that, in a performative effect, becomes a commonplace of Chinese society.

Dynamism and rationality

The 'average' Chinese, who has achieved 'small prosperity' (*xiaokang*), is defined as a modern individual: educated, polite and civilised. His or her taste for consumption excludes excess and instinct; he or she knows how to save to buy sophisticated consumer durables. Her relative, reasonable enrichment is due exclusively to her personal qualities: skills, work, honesty, dynamism, 'spirit of change'. Compared with the excesses of the nouveaux riches, the dishonesty of millionaires who owe their success to their 'scheming', the middle class is presented as a stratum that respects the law and enjoys no initial privileges.

This flattering portrait forgets to mention that their main advantage is privileged access to education, a university degree being a gateway to the middle class for many. It also omits their other exclusive resources: the social and, possibly, political networks that they naturally construct in the course of their studies and professional activities, both at home or abroad. These resources can be multiplied through clubs, associations or simple informal gatherings, of which the middle classes are fond. Another advantage is the positive social image they enjoy, the legitimacy often attached to their success—what might be called reputational capital—which they exploit to the full, particularly in their conflicts with the authorities.

Political dynamism and stability

Chinese society also sees the middle stratum as a buffer zone— a refuge for those who may have fallen in social status, but more importantly a reception area for the upwardly mobile. It therefore constitutes an essential tool of social order—all the more so in that its political behaviour is marked both by civic dynamism and by an undoubted political conservatism. It has civic dynamism in the sense that social protest movements often involve the middle class, or are supported by a section of it. It is thought to defend its interests and rights vigorously, without neglecting the collective interest in the process. In terms of political conservatism, the middle class is generally opposed to elections and radical solutions to resolve conflicts. It is therefore a politically ideal class: not sufficiently powerful to impose its views, but sufficiently strong to make them known and to represent a driving force in the gradual, measured 'modernisation' of the political system.[9]

A class that is hard to define

The project of constructing a middle class obviously runs into numerous difficulties. The most important concerns its definition. If we agree to regard it as the result of the emergence of two repellent classes (rural labourers and the rich), its contours emerge fairly clearly. The middle classes comprise all those who are and/or feel different from 'peasants'—by education, job, lifestyle—and from the elites—by their tendency to earn money exclusively through hard work and personal talents. Beyond this minimal definition based on a form of class struggle, things get complicated.

One of China's peculiarities is that the 'new middle class'— that of technicians and engineers—does not succeed the old middle class—that of small shopkeepers, artisans, and other intermediate layers. The two emerged at virtually the same time and advanced in tandem. If we place individual entrepreneurs in the same category as administrative staff and, above all, technicians, the general picture of the middle class deviates from the ideal image. The lifestyles and the social and political imaginaries of these categories reveal great contrasts.

There are enormous differences in lifestyle between the minor civil servant, the head of communications in a large enterprise, the university professor and the artist. In reality, the social image projected of the middle class is modelled, explicitly or implicitly, on that of the most 'with-it' fringe of Chinese society—those working in the media, advertising, communications, foreign enterprises, and so forth. The expression of personality, of subjectivity, is not only common practice in this milieu, but a necessity: the need to distinguish oneself in an environment marked by competition and ambition. Likewise, fashionable discourse asserting the superiority of logics of 'being' over 'having' prevails in this social group. One prioritises the equivalent of a 'culture of self' (in Chinese *xiuyang*: cultivating oneself, realising oneself) by engaging in certain sporting or artistic activities, or quite simply by improving one's general culture. The personal project (working for a few years and then 'enjoying life' or travelling, completely changing one's professional orientation, etc.) prevails, at the expense of any reference to a career. Obviously, for most of these 'trendies', the reality is different. Marriage, indebtedness, and the hazards of professional existence often restore people to reason. Nevertheless, this imaginary runs through the group as a shared reference to an ideal, idealised fate that shapes behaviour. Nourished on the ideology (and illusions) of democracy, 'they don't want to be pushed around' like migrants or the destitute. They are ready to defend their interests.

The rest of the middle classes exhibit very different characteristics. Individual entrepreneurs have neither the economic independence—all their activities still depend on administrative authorisation and the good will of the local authorities— nor the social legitimacy—they are assimilated to a lower stage of China's modernisation, the start of the market economy in the 1980s—required for self-assertion as a category. They invariably rely on discretion and direct arrangements. The 'administrative staff' are no differently placed. They are certainly near to the sources of power, and exploit this amply in terms of social and political resources. Nevertheless, their 'traditional' lifestyle and lack of independence—most work in government departments or large Chinese enterprises—strips them of any dissenting margin of manoeuvre.[10]

The 'ideal', 'representative' fringe of the middle class therefore only represents a very small percentage of the population. If we consider the set of characteristics that supposedly define it—income, profession, educational level, as well as lifestyle and political imaginary—it is hard to believe that this group exceeds 5 per cent of the whole population, or fewer than 60 million people. For the most part they are concentrated in the big townships and cities and thus weigh rather more than their actual mass. But the immense responsibility that is China's modernisation would appear to rest on decidedly narrow shoulders.

4

A SOCIETY OF INDIVIDUALS
IN A TIME OF REFORMS

In the case of contemporary China, questions asked by students or the public are often Manichaean in form. This is the price to pay for the domination of the modernisation paradigm in China studies. Has society remained traditional or, on the contrary, embarked on modernity? Has 'communism' retained its influence over people's minds or, on the contrary, have they been freed from the grip of 'power'? Violence has diminished markedly. Why, then, do the Chinese comply with orders? Sometime the questions focus on specific points. Are the young free to choose their spouse? Is love the basis of the couple or is the latter still formed on the premeditated, social selection of a partner? Is sexual freedom now an established fact? Whatever the question, it involves assessing the route to be followed to the Holy Grail of modernity, where people supposedly no longer allow themselves to be taken in by official propaganda, where everyone can rely on their identity as an 'absolute subject' to take their fate into their own hands and on their own talents to succeed, where the past is now mere folklore.

Yet, historians and social scientists dealing with so-called 'developed' or 'modern' societies have argued extensively that modernisation process is a myth. In 'modern' societies, the relations between liberty versus submission, new versus old, democracy versus authoritarianism, reason versus irrationality, are much more complex than postulated by modernisation theories. In individuals' and groups' behaviours it is generally very difficult to call them new or old. What we call tradition is often something that is invented to create new feelings and representations—the nation for example. Who can reasonably believe that in such societies the individual chooses 'in complete freedom', on the basis exclusively of their 'subjectivity', their spouse, profession, political opinions, lifestyle, and behaviour? The unity of this entity—the 'individual'—can hardly be taken for granted. How to combine cultural globalisation and the absolute subject? Likewise, the autonomy of society, the existence of a 'civil society' clearly distinguished from 'power', does not withstand analysis, when we see with what ease finance, men, ideas, and structures of domination circulate between various bodies (NGOs, 'grassroots' associations, international organisations, political parties, the state). Finally, we daily observe the importance of the 'past' in the social life of modern societies. Certainly, it is a past that has been invented or reinvented. But it is one that, through its presence (in the forms of the renewal of family bonds, 'communities', memorial sites, 'authentic' districts), determines behaviour and action. How are we to explain the 'return of the religious' all over the world if the road of rationalisation is so ineluctable?

Let us also recall Norbert Elias's views on the relations between individual and society in so-called modern societies.[1] He believed that the West's historical trajectory conferred more and more power on the individual, but that this did not lead to a corresponding diminution in the role of social determinants with respect to these individuals—quite the reverse. The latter unquestionably possess greater 'liberty', in the sense that institutions (the family, the state, etc.) compel them less formally, less violently, and less directly than in the past to choose some particular profession, spouse, or lifestyle. Nevertheless, in the West as in China, this change cannot be interpreted in terms of the triumph of the individual, of 'liberty', because (Elias argues) the socialisation of behaviour has been extended and deepened at the same time. In China too, the individual is more social, more shaped than in the past by his or her relations with their immediate social environment and the imaginaries generated by the media, communication and consumption.[2] To be a strong individual, to be a personality—that is, to release oneself from the power of others and events—assumes a solid grasp of social codes in order to manipulate them to one's advantage, and hence ultimately being subject to their influence. The personality of an asocial individual is never recognised. Having come from nowhere—still highly suspect in the 1980s, they lived frugally, crammed into dormitories, on meagre teacher's salaries—the Chinese artists who today sell their work for hundreds of thousands (even millions) of dollars are pure personalities. However, both in their 'determination' to create and in their capacity to express an era, to understand what is going to 'work', they are utterly 'socialised'. They have identified the spirit of the age and assimilated the operations of society, the market and artistic power in order to establish themselves. Following Michel Foucault, it might be said that they have set themselves norms that they construct in the course of their social experience.[3]

Chinese society has indeed become a 'society of individuals'. Compliance is no longer ensured essentially by violence or repression. The institutions that used to closely control the individual appear to have lost their power. Residents' committees, employers, families in urban areas, clans, notables in the countryside, the Party and the police over the whole territory are no longer supposed to frustrate initiative. The institutions of control must adapt to the new situation and have to employ persuasion, strength of conviction and communication techniques that approximate to those used by the media and advertising. What are the mechanisms, phenomena and ethics that induce individuals to set themselves social norms?

A Society of Subjects of Their Own Existence

Let us go back, first of all, to the upheaval represented by the emergence of the policy of reform and opening up and, in particular, the rise in living standards, to the material existence of the Chinese. Until the start of the 1980s, many urban residents and almost all rural residents possessed neither a bathroom, nor a fridge, nor a TV set. The purchase of a washing machine required an illegal transaction with a foreigner, in order to obtain the currency valid in the famous Friendship stores. Meat was reserved for feast days; the vegetables and fruits were always the same. Restaurants were scarce, state-owned and did not serve after 7pm. Clothing was strictly uniform (quite literally so) and unisex. Furniture was reduced to a minimum. Walking for most, and bicycles for the more fortunate, were the only means of transportation. Material scarcity, and an ascetic morality violently imposed by the authorities, ruled out any personal input into everyday behaviour. Today, not only is the growth in consumer goods exponential, but the opening up of what might be called a 'field of lifestyles' allows everyone to choose their own 'style'.

Paradoxically, this rupture leaves individuals in a great state of confusion because it is occurring in a universe where sociality is more and more intense and subjects less and less isolated. Urban residents increasingly go out, but never alone. During the week, they eat with friends or colleagues. At the weekend, they go on trips to the countryside—informally, with groups containing family members and friends of friends, or, more formally, in clubs of owners of the same make of car. Sports clubs are also sites of intense social activity for the new Chinese. People are all the happier to make contact with old school mates as their reunions extend the network of relations that little bit further.

In its turn, China is confronting the big question: how to be 'oneself'? The answers vary, but have a major impact on individual behaviour. The individual 'freedom' that has been granted, demanded and popularised (notably by the media) is in fact shaped and limited by the constraints entailed by the multiplication of social relations and the increasing importance of communication. In this new world, where people are constantly mixing with strangers (indigenous or otherwise), rules of etiquette are gradually becoming established and social relations are, spontaneously, generators of norms. In new residences, strangers with different social backgrounds have to adopt rules so as to organise (and constrain) the lives of co-owners. Newspapers popularise new behaviours and new tastes that become social norms. The authorities themselves launch campaigns against spitting and anti-social forms of behaviour. The growing number of books and newspaper articles devoted to good manners and social skills, and the constant references in official discourse to improving the character of the population, to the need for the Chinese to be modern, indicate that this work on 'civilising' manners, but also on 'classifying' individuals, is being carried out by the 'government', the media, and the population. Certainly, it is difficult to force people to give up spitting and displaying more or less naked torsos during the hot summer evenings in popular districts of Beijing or Shanghai. But the man in the street rails at the bad driving of his compatriots, their rude attitude, heedless of the requisite politeness, their inability to form a queue, to respect red lights or to behave when they visit foreign countries. In any event, members of the middle class are supposed to assert their identity and distinction through their 'education'.[4] In this exacting context, individuals have to meet expectations but also to exhibit, in the face of competition from others, the specific characteristics of their own ego. These standardised frameworks of behaviour are not imposed through repressive policies but infused painlessly into society.

Effects of Fashion

It is striking that the importance attributed to individual liberty and personal style in the press and among the population, especially the middle classes, is accompanied by a spectacular increase in conformism. It is necessary to follow fashions and conform to a certain image but, at the same time, conformity consists in being original. Individuals have no choice but to distinguish themselves from others and to share with them the same set of behaviours, as well as appearing as outgoing persons respecting the standards of social interaction. The violence of social change, a lack of experience, and an absence of traditions in this area lead to a rapid turnover in fashions. After a few years of radical 'modernism' in the 1980s and the beginning of the 1990s, when contempt for country life and a cult of the city, the consumption of industrial goods and a quest for material enrichment formed the bases of social activity, today we observe a reversion to a certain social tranquillity (people are buying houses in the country), an increasingly marked tendency to 'personal development' (yoga is winning over a lot of enthusiasts), and a yen for authentic, even organic, products. Logics of being must take priority over those of having. People buy old furniture and take an interest in traditions. Modern exegeses of Confucius meet with phenomenal success.

The old virtues are coming back into fashion. People learn management via DVDs in which gurus cite both the canons of Chinese wisdom and the latest developments in marketing. In the countryside, local cults, exorcism and divination are being revived. In the towns and cities, conversions to Protestantism are multiplying, particularly among the middle classes. It takes a few dozen people to create a 'family church' (*jiating jiaohui*) and satisfy their taste for new forms of spirituality. People think of themselves as ecological and respectful of the non-material heritage. Society is reviving traditional feast days, some of them very largely forgotten, and again collecting old porcelain and old furniture. In other words, as in 1980s Europe, in the last few years China has discovered the virtues of 'authenticity' and the modernity of tradition.

This labour of the ego obviously does not take the same form in a journalist on a 'hip' fashion magazine as a dustman or a peasant from the western provinces. But all are entering the field of lifestyles and the necessary competition of personalities. Migration, and the development of trade, television and tourism induce 'stragglers' to conform. The style of female migrant workers, and their way of dressing and behaving, does not deceive 'genuine' fashionable metropolitan women. But it bears virtually no resemblance to that of their compatriots who have remained in the countryside. The fact that the pace of change is slower or more staggered in rural areas does not mean that lifestyles are not developing there. We are witnessing a descending diffusion of behavioural norms, a graduation that aims at different levels of the population while forming part of one and the same development. Similarly, while many attitudes are contradictory—some people buy cars but go to work on foot; others engage in green organisations but travel increasingly often by plane—they are no more so than elsewhere. In every respect, Chinese society is displaying an extremely high level of porosity to both official propaganda and 'trends' in international public opinion.

Social Anxiety

We also note a pronounced sensitivity to social rumours fuelled by a latent sense of insecurity. Chinese people feel they are living in a scary world. There is an enormous gap between the sense of security felt by the average Westerner in China and the fear prevalent among the population. Criminality obviously exists, but it is a far cry from what is experienced elsewhere. Yet the security sector is flourishing. Security doors and bars on windows form part of the environment. Thick walls surround apartment blocks. Almost all of them have uniformed caretakers and the most modern include sophisticated security systems. In conversation, 'danger' is omnipresent, even in the villages, where the natives remind you that 'although there have never been any thefts, you absolutely must lock the car'.

In the case of the generation aged 40 and over, this sense can perhaps be justified in view of the almost complete lack of criminality until the 1980s. From the perspective of that time, the reform period seems terribly dangerous. No doubt it can also be linked to the events that marked the Maoist period. For the young, the decisive element is probably a condition of social anxiety bound up with confronting a changing world that is extremely competitive. It must also be stressed that the young generations have few occasions to fly the family nest. The village, the district and the family still form the sole horizon of most children and adolescents. In rural areas situated less than 60 kilometres from Beijing, most children have never been to the capital. Most students arrive at university without having left their province; all of them without having left China; and many without having spoken to a foreigner. This lack of experience of 'otherness', and over-protectiveness on the part of parents, does not prepare students to face the outside world or perilous situations. Subsequently, they seek to find their place in an unstable world. Amid casual employment, conflicts of love and duty, and an uncertain future entailing big economies, the security of the family nest becomes a happy memory.

Thus, the fragmentation of social space and the visible emphasis on security in China stem both from a habitus established in the 1950s and from more contemporary phenomena. The socialist division into work units, neighbourhoods, communities (*shequ*) and villages, whose boundaries were clearly demarcated and almost impossible to cross, aimed at complete control of everyday life. Today, in a quite different context, this morphology has proven equally adaptable to new needs. It meets the authorities' objectives in terms of social control, but also a desire to belong to a 'we' that guarantees a certain 'living environment'. Everyone can move where they wish, but they will find virtually the same structure of habitation, with a residents' committee, a building management, caretakers, and so on. This is reassuring and corresponds to a widespread norm.

In towns and cities, the retreat of the socialist type social housing in favour of commercial gated communities facilitates the transition. Everyone gains something from this model: elderly couples, for whom there are services and activities onsite, and young couples, who want to preserve their space while feeling safe. Thus, while residents' committees are no longer as intrusive as they used to be, and are obliged to respect people's private lives, they have not entirely lost their function. They continue to monitor, to concern themselves with the 'living environment', to help people in difficulties, to resolve conflicts, and so on. They are widely mobilised during major public events. What is more, in becoming professional, they are evolving towards a form of 'social work', with old activists—old ladies selected by the Party—being replaced or combined with young graduates.

For rural residents, the village or township remains the site of primary identity and the vector of protective relations even in the case of migration. Far from undermining this pattern, the mobile phone makes it possible to mobilise one's network at any point, from the village to the main regions of migration, where compatriots can provide precious information about the labour market.

Sex and Marriage in the (Chinese) City

Apart from universal taboos, sexual practices are completely free. The authorities believe that sexuality is a personal matter and generally respect this principle. Sex before or outside marriage and homosexuality are no longer hounded. Only pornography remains prohibited.

Marriage and marital fidelity are no longer legal obligations but that does not mean that social norms have disappeared. In other terms, the lifting of legal constraints allows free range for the pressure of social norms and moral values. Traditional-socialist norms are far more influential in the countryside than in urban areas. In towns and cities, cohabitation is widespread. As is often the case in matters of sex and romance, the urban space is more open-minded than the countryside. Even so, this openness is highly dependent on the social milieu in which people grow up. More restricted among popular categories, it increases as one rises up the social scale.

There has been little study of sexuality in China. There are a few well-known sexologists and the media has no inhibitions about dealing with the issue, although this is always done tactfully and often in a scientific light. The following analyses are mainly based on interviews with young Chinese people or discussions with Chinese researchers and journalists.

Public morality, social moralities

As is well known, control of bodies is not only the remit of the political authorities. Very often, it simply follows public opinion and, more precisely, those who create it. Thus, high school teachers often intervene when they learn of the existence of sexual relations that are deemed unduly premature or 'disruptive' for pupils. In urban districts, too, a libertine lifestyle involving multiple partners or 'public' adultery may result in the cautious, conciliatory intervention of the residents' committee. In these cases, however, the police are rarely called in. By contrast, sexuality remains suspect in the eyes of the authorities when it might possess a political flavour. This is true of homosexuality. It is respected, but the gay community must remain discreet. As in the case of religion or social protest, any institutionalisation of the phenomenon remains suspect.

'Traditional' morality or, at any rate, the morality that prevailed after 1949, remains pervasive, but not excessively so. Choice of partner is free in principle, but, once chosen, the couple must be exclusive, including sexually. Divorce is permitted in cases of serious disagreement and remarriage completely normal. An inquiry conducted among students at Tsinghua University indicates that the sex life of couples must be balanced (neither too much, nor not enough) and must satisfy both partners. However, marriage remains a serious business. People must be in love or at least present themselves as such but the basis of marital happiness is not love or even feelings, but 'accord', 'harmony' and a 'good understanding' between the partners. Social endogamy is important. Differences of condition between the spouses—financial, professional or cultural—should not be unduly great; and, where they do exist, should be in favour of the husband. In short, marriage is a multi-criterion affair to which the students devote a good deal of time, energy and thought.

That said, social milieus also diverge from the model. In the countryside, not only is homosexuality 'unthinkable', but non-arranged marriages are rare. Migration is nevertheless altering things. In 'hip' circles (artistic, journalistic, etc.), cohabitation is commonplace, homosexuality advertised, 'passionate' relationships prioritised. In other social strata or situations (such as the search for a spouse via classified ads), the demands are less romantic. They are precisely defined in terms of annual income, profession, level of education, and geographical origin. But such attitudes prompt criticism. In universities, lecturers explain to students that marriage is a matter of feelings, the meeting of minds, and certainly not social milieu. Radio programmes respond to the anxieties of youth by explaining that well-being is not simply material.

In short, while opinions and practices differ, coupledom, and the married couple, remains a safe option, including among homosexuals, some of whom demand the right to marry. Celibacy is something to be endured, especially among young women who, once over the age of thirty, are afraid of not 'getting hitched' and missing out on a normal life. An exclusive couple, which must satisfy all desires (sexual, reproductive, social, lifestyle)—such is the model. But how to achieve it? That is the big question that preoccupies the young generations.

Normalising freedoms

As in 'developed societies', sex is at the centre of a highly ambiguous 'liberating' discourse. It might be said that sex has invaded the public stage. Censorship certainly also operates in

---

BEING GAY IN CHINA

There are bars, nightclubs, and lesbian, gay, bisexual and trans-gender associations. Some activity in favour of gay marriage—a mini-gay pride—has occurred in Beijing. Articles are devoted to the problems faced by homosexuals. Every year, a law legalising homosexual marriage is proposed to the National People's Congress—hitherto without success. Some gay groups are associated with AIDS prevention work. But all this is monitored and snuffed out when the possibility of 'gay power' seems to emerge, when the demands become (or seek to be) more obtrusive, or when the reputation of the Chinese nation is at stake. In January 2010, the election of a Chinese 'Mr Gay' was prohibited.

Aside from the fact that the political field is closed to them, Chinese gays are not in a radically different situation from that prevailing in many so-called developed countries. Generally accepted, gays must put up with sarcastic remarks and incomprehension as soon as they quit 'advanced' social milieus. Not everyone dares to 'come out of the closet' (*chugui*). Some have understanding parents; for others it is quite a shock. What is certain is that the average parent prefers a 'normal' child, especially at a time of a one-baby policy when a grandchild is a rare, precious thing. There is no religious taboo in these moral judgements. Homosexuality is not perceived in Judeo-Christian fashion as a sin against morality or God. It is simply something bizarre, abnormal, with respect to the nature of things.[5]

---

this domain. Nude photos are not permitted in magazines. Sex may be spoken about in them, but 'in general', without going into details. It is necessary to be allusive or skirt around unduly direct questions from readers or listeners. But suggestive advertising dominates the urban space; brothels disguised as barbershops and sex shops are to be found in every district; porn is one of the main subjects of interest to internet users, even if it is pursued by the authorities. U.S. series dealing with sex (like

Sex and the City) enjoy great success. In private or small group discussions, it is an important subject.

In these matters, the least that can be said is that the Maoist regime did not prepare the parents of the new generations to have an opinion on the issue. Not that they did not know about sex, but the fact that it was denied, even persecuted, and in any event completely confined to the privacy of marriage and reproduction, makes dialogue with the new generation difficult.

Many young urban residents are 'trying to find themselves' and looking for models. Sexual partners are met via the internet or in night clubs. People 'try out' foreigners and discuss their respective merits. People want to try new things, to have fun, not to marry before having had some experience. Climaxing becomes a norm. Virgins are ridiculed. People go and consult for problems of frigidity, and so on. People want to seduce, lose weight, wear alluring underwear. But such attitudes are not opposed to marriage. Instead, what is involved is a phase, a period of experimentation that does not contradict coupledom, but on the contrary can help 'make it succeed' at a later date. At all events, that is how things are often presented in interviews.

This norm is nevertheless all the more difficult to embrace in that it is opposed to the more classical ones of public morals. It seems that today's couple faces two major problems. The first involves the conflicts that arise between the need for social success and the demands of the ideal of coupledom. Wives want their husbands to succeed and ensure them and their offspring maximum material comfort. The father's role seems to be less educative than economic. Here we notice an astonishing phenomenon. Far from leading to an increase in female work, the putative 'individualism' of modern society prompts a number of women, especially in affluent milieus, to return to the household. Certainly, numerous spouses reject this model and invest in the world of work. But they must reckon with social pressure, especially from grandparents, who believe that a woman's place is in the home caring for the child and supporting her husband's career. Social success is such a central ideal that it demands a kind of division of labour. This pressure on the 'genders' creates tension and frustration in couples.

The second, essentially male problem derives from the contradiction between the desire to marry a virgin and, at the same time, the wish to have an experienced partner. Those who express the desire are not good at justifying it. Aside from any religious taboo, it seems that the main motivation is mundane: it is necessary to have a new, healthy product, especially for the purposes of having a child. This point of view is mocked by some 'liberated' women and by the media, because it presupposes male/female inequality that is far from 'socially correct'. After all, no one demands a virgin husband.

It is easy to appreciate the source of anxiety this requirement represents for the young married woman, and even for the future young married woman. Confidences garnered during private interviews or radio programmes indicate that the first sexual relationship is problematic on account of this exigency of virginity. 'I love X but if I go to bed with him, and he leaves me, how will I be able to find a husband?' Some women turn to remedial surgery, but that cannot restore a good reputation. A young woman whose morals are deemed lax will have difficulty finding a partner prepared to commit himself. She can re-acquire a 'certain virginity' in another place or milieu—a possibility that changes everything—but the issue is treated no less seriously for all that.

In urban areas, it would seem that for many men, but also for a certain number of women, sex is an extra-marital business. In sum, the start of the relationship might be passionate and marked by strong sexual desire. After a while, however, routine, work and obligations reduce libido. People then become partners, associates in a relationship that 'must be harmonious'. Men go to 'look elsewhere', take a mistress or mistresses, and/or visit prostitutes. Furthermore, in some affluent milieus, having one or more maintained mistresses is now a matter of social status. Women react badly to this state of affairs. Cases of suicide, divorce, or conjugal violence often seem to have male adultery as their immediate cause.

The situation is doubtless different in rural areas. Sexuality there seems to play a marginal role compared with the cities. But its role can nevertheless be assessed indirectly by reference to the prevalent AIDS epidemic. The prostitution that flourishes along the main highways, fuelled in part by people on journeys but also in part by local consumption, suggests that marriage is not the only place that sexual activity takes place in rural China.

Children

As we can see, analysis of sexuality in terms of freedom versus determination does not withstand comparison with actual practice for long. It also emerges fairly rapidly that the tradition/modernity opposition does not enable us to account for the subtleties of the current 'configurations' of sex. The same is true when it comes to the situation of children.

The birth rate poses an immediate problem in urban areas. Single progeny is a heavily resented imposition and a number of couples do not want children. This is becoming a major problem and the single-child policy is beginning to be seriously challenged. Couples who are both single children can now have two of their own. In some towns and cities, the principle of two children per urban couple is being tested out. Serious thought is being given to allowing determined couples to have a second child in order to limit the long-term impact of the single-child policy on demographics.

The norm of social success, social selection by education, and geographical status determine the fate of the juvenile age group from the outset. On the one hand, there are children living in rural areas whose educational prospects end at best at high school. On the other, there are the offspring of urban residents who go to university in growing proportions—something like three-quarters. It is well-known that education systems that are free and open to all still reproduce social 'distinctions' and inequalities, but in China, the situation is worse, because there are legal barriers to higher education. Most children living in rural areas cease their studies at the end of the nine years of compulsory education and do not go to high school. Their only prospect is to swell the ranks of the migrants who in coming years will go to settle permanently (but at a rate impossible to assess) in urban areas.

The stress laid on education, as on segregation of peasants, might be seen as a 'return to tradition'. The renascent Confucian imperative is supposedly vigorously reasserting an 'aristocratic', circular conception of education: education alone can form the elite, but only the latter can be educated. However, the imperative of education might equally be regarded as a requirement of the contemporary world, of the imaginary of the knowledge economy, of the need for ever-higher qualifications to obtain a job. All development theories make much of education, opening up access to schools, and competition between talents and forms of training. Similarly, the existence of the barriers to the entry of rural residents can be analysed as the result of a desire to grant a monopoly on success to one, albeit large, social stratum, which is deemed educated and modern. Once this social stratum, supportive of the regime, has been created, it will be time to extend education to a larger proportion of the population—that is, to the children of migrants.

For all that, the life of urban children is no paradise. In fact, the pressure of social success via education leads to terrible suffering. At all levels, competition is fierce. The fight to be in the best classes of the best schools begins as early as primary school (and will soon be from kindergarten, according to popular jokes) as the best primary schools provide access to the best high schools and hence to the greatest chances of success. After school, parents impose additional courses. Even non-scholarly activities are taken seriously very early on. If not cut out to be an Einstein, a child might become a famous footballer or a virtuoso. He or she will therefore have to train daily or practice their instrument for two or three hours a day. Some are entrusted to grandparents or sent to boarding school for a more effective education. Failure, inability to pass the entry exam for university, entry into a poor university, or, worse still, early educational problems all represent a catastrophe. The increased consumption of drugs or growing addiction to video games among youth seems to derive in part from the emergence of a category of urban residents who are educational failures. There are few prospects for this kind of pupil. Professional training is underdeveloped and most 'physical' professions (building, the hotel industry, catering, beauty treatment, hairdressing) are the domain of migrants. For the wealthiest, there remains study abroad, which makes it possible to circumvent selection via education. Many Chinese students who go abroad have not passed the *gaokao*, or have been unsatisfactorily placed. This explains the significant failure rate among them: most are no better prepared for this second chance, which requires them to learn a foreign language.

This obstacle race is based on very strict educational criteria. It involves absorbing the maximum amount of knowledge and regurgitating it by answering series of simple questions. High school teachers like disciplined but lively pupils, who work hard, have an excellent memory, and who are very involved in social activities.

At university, things become even more complex. Students are asked to have an opinion or, at any rate, to argue a point of view. Professors want diligent pupils, who also have a personality. Pedagogical discourse is very marked (practice less so) by the idea of abandoning conformism, breaking the repetitive, copy-cat logic of Chinese-style education. The criticism that foreign enterprises often level at skilled Chinese personnel—heads stuffed full of facts, but not good minds, good at obeying not at taking initiatives—is probably justified in most cases. Students are therefore faced with the need to be good educationally and at the same time to demonstrate personal qualities, to be singular individuals. Finally, they are asked to exhibit signs of personality and a spirit of initiative in social activities (student associations, placements in NGOs, participation in artistic activities, Party cells, etc.), which are defined and controlled by the university. The norm is to be original.

THE RELATIONSHIP TO WORK

In the world of work as well, everyone is required to be both submissive and innovative. These paradoxical imperatives induce in many Chinese an ambiguous attitude towards private life. The latter occupies considerable space compared with the Maoist era, since much of what happens within the family escapes the eye of power. However, most people believe that it is increasingly impossible for them to erect a barrier between their personal life and work. The migrant housed by his employer, the journalist harassed by his editor, the 'cadre' who takes work home with him, and so on, are always more or less constantly in the world of work. Little attention is paid to labour productivity, the important thing seeming to be devotion to the task and demonstrating that one is always available. The importance of social activities also contributes to this phenomenon. After work, people go to eat or have a drink with colleagues. When there is no overtime to be done, it is not unusual to go out at the weekend with a group of friends some of whom are neighbours at the office or in the workshop. It is as if there was no separation between work and leisure.

5

THE POLITICAL PUZZLE

Compared with the aspects of Chinese reform that we have just looked at, the political sphere seems easier to deal with. Analysts like counter-posing an unsatisfied but submissive society to an intransigent, static government, on the one hand, and a courageous but weak dissidence, on the other. Cultural and economic modernity supposedly contrast with the political conservatism of a 'power' that does not want to let go of anything, and which exploits 'nationalism' to fill the vacuum once occupied by the great socialist project. According to Andrew Nathan, the absence of democracy is due to the capacity of Party bureaucrats to adapt to modernity without changing the political regime: China is in the grip of 'authoritarian resilience'.[1] In this view, China is like the victim of a syndrome that prevents it liberating itself from its past. As such, authoritarian resilience is useful for describing but not for analysing what is going on, on the political scene. The true question is how authoritarian resilience resists change.

Certainly, political parties are prohibited. Associations completely independent of government are only tolerated in exceptional cases and must 'return to the fold' or disappear once they reach a certain size. Nevertheless, the thesis of 'authoritarian resilience' has difficulty accounting for a number of phenomena that reveal very important changes in power relations. However, these changes can be only perceived if we assume with Foucault that 'power is not something that is acquired, seized or shared … power is exercised from innumerable points, in the interplay of nonegalitarian and mobile relations'.[2]

First of all, there are institutional changes, which range from the building of a new legal system, via significant liberalisation as regards freedom of the press and speech, to the 'professionalisation' of political personnel. Next, a proliferation of social movements, which affect a sizeable number of sectors, sits ill with the image of an 'amorphous' society. Finally, the emergence of numerous debates among the elites and in the media about the country's political future, the role that the middle class might play in it, and the place already occupied by nation-state building, demonstrates that China's trajectory remains linked to the Western 'model'. 'Nationalism' does not appear to be a simple formula intended to silence stirrings of protest, but one of the resources of the imaginary of the Chinese nation. We can find elements of 'authoritarian resilience' that limit the degree of democratisation of the society in many countries.

In order to assess this seemingly contradictory situation, we shall once again have to free ourselves of a mythology. This time, it is that of 'democratisation'—a supposedly ineluctable linear process that leads, via social movements and the struggle for liberty and universal suffrage, to 'society' triumphing over 'power'. The crisis is resolved and the universal laws of political modernity are imposed on power.

Once released from this mythology, the Chinese situation appears much less far removed from the problematic of democratisation experienced by most European countries. There too, it involved the elites giving a form to popular representation without lapsing into chaos or losing power, finding common ground with society so that it could choose competent masters.

And 'democratisation' is just as much a result of policies from above, aimed at modernising the domination of the elites and rendering it more effective, as the product of action from 'below', seeking to confer more power on social interests. As in the case of many countries that are democratic today, the process of trial-and-error is long and hesitant; and regressions form part of it. Democratisation is a trajectory that is always particular and which can be challenged at any point.

It must also be remembered that sheltering behind the word 'democratisation' is a scattered set of realities. Democracy can be a system of representation, but it can also be a way of managing (and controlling) social conflicts while guaranteeing public liberties. Finally, it can be social, affording citizens a system of social security and access to education. This does not necessarily all go together. India is doubtless a great representative democracy, but in terms of social policies, it is light years behind China.

A Moderate Pluralism

In China, the political field, while not democratic, is no less dynamic for that. Certainly, the rulers are not chosen through competitive elections and freedom of expression and association are highly restricted. Nevertheless, the landscape has nothing in common with the Mao years. Censorship has decreased measurably, elections occur, and the political apparatus allows some room for professionalisation and the expression of pluralism.

The Internet Revolution and its Limits

As in every country in the world, the development of the internet and the media in general have considerably altered the relations between citizens and the ruling strata.[3] Scandals are

107

constantly denounced; blogs invade the web and mobilise the population; and the whole international press is at the fingertips of internet users. Censorship is ineffectual. Those who wish to inform themselves are past masters in the art of evading it. Only, like everywhere else, the internet has its limits. Those who expected it to give rise to an oppositional 'citizens' conscience' have been disillusioned. Most internet users are interested in game sites and on-line sales, pornographic films, or 'lifestyle' blogs. It is certainly easier now for activists to mobilise the population over a case of pollution, an affair connected with food safety, or bureaucratic malfeasance. But, as in the case of newspapers, such scandals are issues that pit sections of the bureaucracy and different interests against one another and do not challenge the regime. The struggle against pollution and corruption are official causes. As for the rest, the internet can lead a horse to water, but cannot make it drink.

Furthermore, the development of the internet reduces its credibility and reveals its dangers. The proliferation of false rumours and the positions adopted by the international press during recent political events (Tibet, Olympic Games, arrests of dissidents) make Chinese users suspicious. False denunciations and revelations about the private lives of some people have resulted in cases of suicide. Manhunts have been organised through the internet, sometimes targeting people who were innocent. Such excesses lead many Chinese citizens to think about the need to erect legal barriers and set up rules of the game for netizens.

Finally, the internet is a weapon that can be used by anyone, including the government. Local bureaucracies are encouraged to 'communicate', to fight against rumours and enemies of the Party. Every bureaucracy has employees whose work is to read what is said about government policies and politicians' behaviours on websites and social networks that are viewed as the

MULTIPLE STANDARDS IN CENSORSHIP

In the private or academic sphere, one can say anything—or virtually anything. Anti-government diatribes pour from the mouth of the man in the street. Nevertheless, speaking out publicly is much more risky. The list of taboo subjects has diminished considerably, but it exists and is resolutely respected: independence for Taiwan and the peripheral territories, for example, or a multi-party system. Dissidents know what to expect. Aside from these subjects, censorship obviously exists, but it is diffuse, halting, and therefore sometimes violent, often imprecise, and generally ineffective. Appointees wielding scissors have been reduced to 'assessing' articles or artworks subjectively and hence uncertainly.

Newspapers obviously benefit from this monitored freedom—and this is for two very different reasons. The first stems from the 'marketisation' of the economy. The media are now press groups that must make money and therefore attract readers by publishing credible, appealing news. This reduces the role of stereotypical language correspondingly. Conversely, they must not unduly upset investors and advertisers. A second phenomenon: the media have not only become vehicles for expressing opinions and exposers of scandals, but also an issue in political struggles. The arrest of a journalist certainly shows that the media are not independent, but above all it indicates that the political factions that supported him, and allowed him to publish disconcerting articles, have lost a battle (although maybe not the war). The quality of the news published in the press is such that the specialist, as soon as he or she can read Chinese, no longer needs to go to China to follow current events.

The media therefore play it by ear. One can talk about sex, but in an allusive fashion and not excessively; religion is no longer out of bounds, but must remain a private affair; 'lifestyles' are a legitimate subject; a particular scandal can be denounced once the denounced faction is incapable of mounting opposition. In short, the information available is the product of accommodations between the desire to inform, logics of mind control, economic profitability (and reader satisfaction), and political

109

ambitions. Very often, the fate of an article, newspaper or jour-nalist depends on contingent factors. A person or group who manages to persuade the powerful that an article is a threat to the country's stability and reputation; an abrupt political clamp-down due to an unforeseen eventuality; a subject that becomes taboo for some unknown reason—these are so many events that can result either in a brutal resumption of control over the media or in a relaxation, by definition temporary and non-insti-tutionalised, of controls.

only place where the public can express their opinion. In addi-tion, the authorities have financial and technical resources not possessed by mere mortals. There is talk of people specifically paid by the government to write laudatory commentaries on discussion sites. The police can flood news websites with advantageous content.

In other words, and contrary to some people's illusions, the internet cannot trigger the revolution or ensure order. It can merely facilitate mobilisation and reveal secrets—or render official discourse more effective—it is a form of media.

Elections and Electors

Contrary to expectations, for the time being economic growth has not led China to representative democracy. Moreover, unlike what occurred in European countries in the nineteenth century, we have not witnessed the emergence of an electoral system based on qualification (level of education, payment of taxes, etc..) limited to the 'advanced'. On the contrary, peas-ants are the only citizens who have a (very limited) right to vote: since the start of the 1980s villagers have been allowed to choose their leaders by universal suffrage. The objective was not to promote democracy as such, but to renew the notables and, in particular, eliminate the most corrupt, brutal and incompetent—in other words, to add popular legitimacy to bureaucratic legitimacy. The initiative may now be deemed a success. Today, the great majority of villagers choose their village head. Certainly, electoral procedures are variable. Frequently, there is no electoral campaign; voting by show of hands is not uncommon; the ballot boxes go walkabout or are not monitored; the election of people not to the liking of the higher authorities is annulled, and so forth. People are usually not very interested in participating in elections unless they can be used as a way to get rid of a bad leader. But, in addition to the fact that this is generally the case wherever universal suffrage is introduced,[4] it must be admitted that the original objective has been achieved. Village tyrants have often disappeared; we witness the appearance of a new generation of heads—sometimes the sons of the previous ones, members of influential families, but more modern, more educated, and more capable of contributing to local prosperity. As for 'outsiders', when they are reasonable—in other words, when they find common ground with the local bureaucracy—they are integrated into the Party and the administrative apparatus.[5] Finally, it should be recalled that elections rarely lead to revolution, being more a stabilising factor than a vehicle for political change.

But institutional development stops there, far removed from what many observers hoped. Democratisation only involves areas where big politics are not involved. Village affairs come down to domestic matters—the 'management' of economic and social interests by the authorities—and completely exclude questions that are political in Arendt's sense of the term: the principles of living together in society and the form of government.[6] Furthermore, even if, officially, village elections seem to be a stage in a gradual apprenticeship in democracy by the whole population, the vote has not been extended to the cities.

Experiments are conducted on some estates Party; secretaries are sometimes elected from a list containing more candidates than posts; people continue to choose the members of residents' committees, who have already been selected by the Party. No large-scale reform is envisaged that would radically transform the political landscape. The authorities are clearly not convinced that the good citizens China already possesses—informed urban residents—would restrict themselves in their choice exclusively to economic and social management and be capable of unity. Paradoxically, peasants, with their 'common sense', seem more reliable when it comes to having their say in local affairs. But would that still be the case if it came to choosing national leaders? Are these initial democratic steps going to end up in an uncontrollable situation if they are extended? On this point, the authorities and the enlightened urban population are at one: in a situation of universal suffrage, the rural vote, which is still largely majoritarian, risks being prey to every kind of political adventure, religious fundamentalism, populist manipulation, and all kinds of interference from the power of money. These fears are the same as those that gripped the big and petty bourgeoisie of Europe when faced with the rising power of the popular will.

A Thermidorian and Technocratic Elite

Routinisation and normalisation of procedures and an increasingly salient role for collegiality in decision-making processes are evident in government. The first thing we observe is a professionalisation of political personnel. Civil servants are now largely recruited through competitive exams and there has been a considerable rise in the educational level of leading figures. Even the privileged children of the older leaders, the 'princelings', must obtain a degree to further their administrative or business careers (a foreign one is the crowning achievement). Expertise is the channel via which those with intellectual capital accede to the elite. Legal procedure is now essential in the exercise of power. Courts are more independent and death sentences must be approved by the Supreme People's Court. Lawyers are gaining moderately in influence. The revolution is silent and gradual, but nevertheless significant. It does not preclude arrangements or circumvention, but 'routinises' and stabilises political power. In other words, arbitrariness is in retreat and power is becoming more predictable.[7]

Yet the position of the individual in the system is no more assured than it was before the reforms. The tyrants have largely disappeared from the political universe. Since the death of Deng Xiaoping, China has entered a period of peaceful, formal succession, in which power is officially bicephalous (Party Secretary/Prime Minister). From Jiang Zemin/Zhu Rongji via Hu Jintao/Wen Jiabao to Xi Jinping/Li Keqiang, selected in 2012–13, leaders have changed regularly every ten years and are chosen collectively. Moreover, national leaders are no longer omnipotent and cannot deviate from the tracks of bureaucratic routinisation. Decisions are taken collectively and therefore involve rough accommodations between different interests and views. At lower levels of government, we find the same phenomenon. Power is collective and individuals are never owners of it. They can use (and sometimes abuse) it, but they can also be stripped of it at any moment, whether in a regular or a brutal fashion. Disgrace is no longer at the behest of one man or the result of an abrupt political turn; it too is the fruit of a collective decision. In this regard, the case of Bo Xilai, purged in 2012, is revealing. One of the regime's principal figures was eliminated from one day to the next without it occasioning any difficulties. Consensus takes precedence.

To shore up their position, the elites will seek to endow their power with a legal, rational, legitimate dimension so as to guarantee a smooth process of social reproduction. Revolutionary legitimacy, which was based on arbitrary violence, great mass movements and charismatic power, is over and done with. Today, it is a question of managing society rationally. In this respect, the elites are in perfect accord with the concepts defended by international organisations and orthodox, normative political thought. Good governance must be promoted and ensured by well-trained, competent and honest civil servants. Policy decisions must be the fruit of rational reflection and arbitration based on scientific techniques. Of course, the control of representative democracy is wanting. But this 'detail' can be justified in technocratic terms. Universal suffrage can result in aberrant choices, political impasses and irrational decisions. Representative democracy is a source of the unpredictable and, from the standpoint of modernisation, dangerous excesses. The international supporters of good governance cannot but be susceptible to this line of argument. The world over, we hear the same refrain from politicians and technocrats: are the people best placed to know what is in their interests? Let us recall that the victory of the 'no' vote in the referendum on the European Constitution in France and the Netherlands led many politicians and political scientists to argue it was definitely not a good idea to ask the opinion of the people on such an important matter.

CORRUPTION AND POLITICS

How is corruption in China to be measured? If we attend to what is said about it in the Western media, it is one of the country's most serious ills. Corruption is allegedly ubiquitous and has dramatic consequences in all fields, including politics. On this assumption, the conclusion dictates itself: long live corruption! Why? Because it has enabled China to experience a record period of growth and the Chinese to enjoy a spectacular rise in living standards.

When people refer to corruption, they are in fact talking about very different things. First of all, they are referring to 'string-pulling'—a phenomenon that is scarcely peculiar to China. Here there is only a problem of degree. On account of the importance of personal relations in social mechanisms, it emerges, altogether logically, that social capital plays a much more important role in Chinese society than, for example, German society. By contrast, in a comparison with Italian society the differences are considerably reduced or even cancelled out. In China, Bribes are generally regarded by civil servants as 'commissions'—just recompense for their contribution to enriching individuals and the nation. To put it another way, in their view additional bonuses are justified by the decisive role of the bureaucracy in economic growth—civil servants are also managers of the local economy—and the low level of their salaries. Reasonable compensation, spent sensibly, does not violate the rules of decency. It is tolerated as long as it is moderate, benefits a group rather than a single individual, does not result in accidents or scandal and does not threaten the health and safety of Chinese people. 'Real corruption', the kind that shocks people (including the moderately corrupt), is excessive corruption—the individual profiteering that has dramatic consequences and leads to riotous expenditure. The really corrupt person, the one who is fingered and jailed, is someone responsible for a scandal (adulterated food, accidents due to negligence, spending money in the brothels and casinos of Macao), someone who has not redistributed his gains, or someone who has not included the people he should have among beneficiaries of his windfall. In any event, that is how the revelation of most affairs is to be interpreted. Some have 'gone beyond the limits' and aroused jealousy. Some have not rationally reinvested the money they have misappropriated. In this context, corruption is not anti-economic. On the contrary, it facilitates transactions in what is still a rigid institutional framework and generates inequalities. Here we come back to the principles of the political economy of the reforms: strong growth that profits everyone, but some more than others. It is a vector of the mutual formation of state and market. The administration allows enterprises to prosper and, in return, enterprises must help civil servants to improve their everyday life and government departments to perform their tasks more efficiently.

Another paradox: often classed among the most corrupt countries in the world, China is unquestionably also the one where punishment of corruption is most severe. For some years, the governors of provinces, the mayors of very large towns, and civil servants at ministerial level have been punished, even sentenced to death. This does not prevent bribes and special favours continuing to flourish, or characters involved in scandals escaping punishment thanks to protection. Everything depends on the political situation and on cadres' behaviours. As in other aspects of social life, it is necessary to have a broad network of relations.

Because of its impact on public opinion and the legitimacy of the regime, accusations of corruption also serve to settle disputes among the elites. Thus, in 2009, Bo Xilai, the governor of Chongqing, 'cleaned up' the municipality with brutal efficiency in order to look like a potential Party Secretary, before himself being purged under the accusation of … corruption.

Be that as it may, Western businessmen discreetly vaunt the virtues of Chinese-style corruption compared with the situation in other countries. In China, once the relevant sum has been agreed, there are no surprises. This demonstrates that even the illegal and the illegitimate do not escape a certain form of institutionalisation.

Finally, we must also take account of the phenomena of political co-option of the elites. Chambers of commerce, associations created by branches of industry, are not official bodies, but are sites of negotiation, enhancement of social capital, and social recognition of businessmen.[8] The development of the Chinese Communist Party is proceeding in the same direction. Some believe that it has not changed and that it is a real site of a form of power that is still just as authoritarian. Others focus on the way its schools are training the country's elites. It is also sometimes said that the Party no longer possesses any real influence, or in any event no real future, because of the increasingly strong leverage of the economy and money. Each of these judgements has its share of truth and make the significance of the membership most puzzling. The Party—more than 83 million members in 2012—remains a key actor in political life, but has changed profoundly. It has accepted into its ranks numerous businessmen, small and large, and not a few intellectuals. The middle class prospers in it. It remains a prerequisite for many careers, be they political, economic or academic. Many grassroots members do not gain much other than respectability from joining. Membership is also a way of protecting oneself when adopting critical positions. People test out their ideas in a small circle; they are permitted to say unwelcome things because the debate has been endorsed in the small world of the 'comrades'. However, if we are to believe the 'democratising' trend in the Party over the last few years, it seems that they should have more power over policy decisions in the future. Giving power to a group of handpicked citizens is another way of changing China, without changing the regime.[9]

However, all these reforms and all these phenomena have not led to the complete integration of the elites. On the contrary, assimilation does not betoken unification, but re-composition along new fault lines. The reforms have shattered the elites into a multitude of groups, regional interests, bureaucratic factions, or lobbies. It is therefore necessary to find compromises that make it possible to maintain equilibrium, and even a certain consensus, which will exclude some protagonists.

Social Protest

The discontent expressed by the man in the street manifests itself vigorously on the stage of social protest. Let us venture a list that makes no claim to be exhaustive: peasants protesting against cases of illegal expropriation or polluting factories; workers unhappy with their dismissal or 'relocation'; city-dwellers mobilising against the meagreness of the sum received in compensation for their eviction; residents poisoned by a contaminated river; migrants overexploited or cheated by dishonest employers; plaintiffs who are the victims of a corrupt civil servant, and so forth. One of the major problems in analysing these movements consists in the tendency to subsume them under a common rubric—challenges to the regime—and to contrast them absolutely with 'power'. Protestors united by a common cause are the good guys, while the rulers are the baddies. All the energies of this 'society', supposedly one and indivisible, are directed towards affirming the law and democratisation—principles to which 'power' is opposed in principle.

However, in his time, Foucault alerted to us to the fact that 'there is no binary and all-encompassing opposition between rulers and ruled at the root of power relations', maintaining that 'where there is power, there is resistance, and yet, or rather, consequently, this resistance is never in a position of exteriority in relation to power'.[10] The employment of a Foucaultian optic sheds very interesting light on social movements in contemporary China, as regards their diversity and the complex relationship between 'society' and 'power' in this sphere.

Diversity of protests

What occurs in China is not protest, but protests. Thus, there is little in common between demonstrations by peasants who have come to work in towns, those by dismissed workers, and defensive actions by flat-owners. Everything differentiates them: interests, status, objectives, methods. Let us start with the social status of the participants. Peasants/workers come from the lowest strata of society. In coming to sell their labour-power, they do not have a sense of serving as labour to be exploited at will by the Chinese miracle, but, on the contrary, of climbing a few rungs on the social scale. Poorly educated, they are regarded as second-class citizens by the authorities and urban population alike, and must resort to forms of solidarity essentially based on geographical or family origin. While their symbolic capital is negligible, for some years they have enjoyed a much better image, on the one hand because their contribution to the economic miracle has to be recognised, and on the other because they now form a not insignificant part of the urban population. Workers dismissed in the 1990s and, more generally, members of lower strata with urban status, retain some small advantages, notably in terms of social policies. As people of urban stock, they retain—albeit decreasingly—a certain small symbolic capital. As for flat-owners, they represent the archetype of the middle class. Issuing from an urban milieu, well-educated, with civilised manners, they hold high-level jobs and enjoy corresponding remuneration.

The demands of these three sections of the population have little in common. For the first, it is predominantly a question of reacting to extreme practices by employers: non-payment of wages, refusal to pay overtime, living or working conditions deemed unacceptable. The state is not a target; what is involved is a classical conflict between labour and capital. By contrast, the second attacks the state, because it was the state that, until recently, guaranteed them a job and decent quality of life. Urban workers were long the apple of the regime's eye. For the third, the issue is asserting the rights of a new social class, based on respect for property and the dignity of the person, a 'just' tax system, protection of the environment and legitimate wealth. Its targets are petty bureaucrats and real estate lobbies, who are accused of incompetence, dishonesty and backwardness.

The means at the disposal of protesters are not of the same kind. While migrant workers have acquired a certain capital in sympathy, by virtue, notably, of a propaganda apparatus that highlights their contribution to growth and the support given to their cause by the intelligentsia, they continue to be treated as 'big children' who must gradually be civilised. Support groups or NGOs are created 'for them'. They lack the organisational resources to make their demands known and to extend their movements, whereas urban workers have a long history of struggling to defend their interests and middle-class movements, whether concerned with the rights of owners or defence of the environment, speak the same language as the authorities. They know how to organise, who makes the decisions, how to get themselves heard and how to manipulate official language, especially when it comes to the rule of law, democracy and modernity.

Finally, the authorities' reaction varies with the nature of the protest. Quick to repress peasant movements, they generally react badly to protests by migrants. Urban workers were treated better. Even if large demonstrations attract the wrath of the police, their demands meet with some sympathy and a fairly systematic effort is made to soften the most dramatic impact of lay-offs. Campaigns against pollution and by homeowners are tolerated as long as they do not overstep the mark or stray from their primary concerns.[11]

We should make it clear that the trade union bureaucracy generally play little role in labour disputes. They remain a transmission belt of the government and they maintain often intimate links with the heads of the relevant enterprises. According to Shen Jie, they have a 'messenger and mediator function'.[12] In the best-case scenario, they limit themselves to creating support funds for laid-off workers and putting in place training for the unemployed. By contrast, it seems that more recently some local trade unions have discreetly got involved in protest movements under both the pressure of workers and the hope of some employers and officials to see the labour disputes solved in a softer and quicker manner.[13]

Likewise, official NGOs have some involvement with protest movements concerned with environmental protection or defending rights (*weiquan*). The idea seems to be preventing unrest and troubles and imposing anti-pollution policies more easily on local bureaucrats.

Power and society: the mixing of genres

The proliferation of protest movements must not be allowed to conceal the fact that the relations between these movements and 'power' have been increasingly fluid since the beginning of the new millennium. Like democratic countries in the past, China seems to be at the beginning of a slow but irresistible process of integrating social protest groups into the mechanics of managing the social.

In the first place, the themes of protest largely coincide with the government's official objectives. Respect for legislation and, in particular, labour law, the legitimation of private property and respect for the environment are an integral part of the discourse of 'power'. In particular, protesters and central government have the same target: the petty bureaucracy. There is a convergence between malcontents, who like the policies but do not see their effects because of bureaucratic resistance, and national leaders, who criticise local cadres for recalcitrance in implementing directives when they threaten their interests. They are united in the utterly technocratic idea that social harmony is imperilled by the practices of the local bureaucracy.

A massive consensus even exists between 'society' and 'power' about the need to change politics without endangering the country's stability by creating an electoral system. In discussions with the man in the street, politicians, or intellectuals, as in the writings of researchers, one gets a sense of distrust of overly radical institutional reforms—in particular, the abrupt introduction of a system of representative democracy. Giving all Chinese citizens the right to vote seems to most of them to be a sensitive issue. The old contempt for rural residents re-emerges on the political terrain. Will peasants prove capable of choosing good leaders and making good decisions? Will they not fall into the hands of unscrupulous groups—gurus, popu-lists of every stripe, local party cliques? Will a democratic gov-ernment bogged down in personal squabbles and interests prove too weak to take the urgent measures required in the social sphere? These are questions raised by rulers and intellec-tuals in European countries in the past. They explain why even the most liberal figures, like the historian Qin Hui or the blogger Han Han, remain cautious about the evolution of the political system. Is it not necessary first to ensure civil liber-ties—freedom of expression and the press, rights to associate and defend interests, an independent legal system—and then wait patiently for prosperity and education to raise the Chinese population to the level required to establish a representative democracy?

The relevant split therefore does not pit the 'social', suppos-edly favourable to complete, immediate democratisation, against the 'political', attached to the continuation of arbitrari-ness. Instead, within government departments, the Party and the different social categories, it divides those who are in favour of an acceleration and institutionalisation of change—more freedom of expression, protest and enterprise—from those who are afraid of it. In the latter group, we can without hesitation range the forces of order (police, army, state security), but also much of the petty bureaucracy. In the former group is to be found a significant fraction of central and provincial govern-ment, but also local cadres who prefer prevention to cure, dia-logue to repression, finding solutions to risking careers.

The general line, which has been applied since the start of the 2000s, favours supporters of a flexible approach to conflict management, although civil liberties have not progressed much as a result. It involves preventing the emergence of social unrest by resolving the problems underlying conflicts. In this domain, the pressure is on the local authorities. Stability has become a criterion for assessing the quality of the work of cadres. In practice, protestors are increasingly attended to and movements decreasingly subject to violent repression. Local authorities have to prevent discontent. When the protesters are sufficiently numerous and determined, social peace is bought, in the literal sense of the word: the authorities distribute money or increase compensation levels. Consequently, a form of escalation has become established among the discontented. As the formula often heard in China puts it: 'If you say nothing, your problem will never be resolved; if you shout a bit, you will get a bit of compensation; if you yell, you will be fully heard.' This syndrome is particularly evident when it comes to land confiscation. It must be said that this is a big issue. According to various sources, the sale of land by local authorities now represents nearly three-quarters of their tax receipts. Every year, around three million peasants lose the right of usufruct of their land.

This 'obligation to negotiate', which encourages the authorities to cede even when the conflict is violent, is illustrated by the affair that ranged the villagers of Wukan (a province of Guandong) against the local authorities in late 2011. A few years earlier, the land in this coastal region was worth nothing and most villagers had abandoned agriculture to go and work elsewhere. More recently, however, numerous projects—in particular, port-related—had conferred considerable value on it and enriched local cadres. The villagers recalled that they were collectively owners of this land and that the authorities were selling it without giving them adequate compensation. Finally, following violent riots and the death of one of the movement's leaders, they were allowed to elect protesters (including the daughter of the deceased) to the new village committee, after the eviction of the old leaders.

Another way of 'managing the social' (*shehui guanli*),[14] without institutionalising procedures and channels for the expression of discontent, consists in permitting the development of NGOs.[15] In 2012, there were nearly 500,000 NGOs. They are active in most spheres: protecting the environment, aiding populations in difficulty, supporting migrants, and so forth. In the main, they are created by government departments, official bodies (trade unions, women's federations, universities), and leading figures or are dependent on them. Some are genuinely independent, but, in that case, they have neither the financial resources nor sufficient *savoir-faire* or enough social capital to exercise any influence. Nevertheless, official NGOs play a not insignificant role. Their existence corresponds to the drastic reduction in the number of civil servants, implying that para-public organisations can take over in certain areas; to the need to deal with problems with greater flexibility than government departments can muster; and, finally, to the need to pressurise local authorities to apply laws and regulations. Their ambiguous position is therefore not an aberration, but corresponds precisely to the formation, without it being institutionalised, of a field of contestation. No procedures, routines or absolute rights exist on which the discontented can rely in order to avoid possible excesses. It is nevertheless possible to mobilise to obtain compensation or benefits by putting pressure on the local or (best of all) the central authorities. Finally, we have to note the existence of an intermediary stratum of NGOs, located between official NGOs and completely independent, yet largely inefficient "genuine"

NGOs. They are affiliated to official institutions but enjoy large room for manoeuvre. They are quite active and efficient organizations and though they help out local governments, they also serve the local communities.

In this context, the treatment of protest varies over time and space. Protests by property-owners are numerous in Beijing and rare in Shanghai. The discontent of migrants is dealt with much better in Shanghai than Guangdong, all the more so in that it is less prevalent in the eastern metropolis than the southern province. Such diversity obviously stems from the attitude of the local authorities, but also from Beijing's desire to be able to dish out repression unimpeded where necessary. At any given moment, the central government can discreetly support protesters according to its own agenda or, on the contrary, prioritise social order.

Intellectuals in No Man's Land

Intellectuals, journalists, lawyers and civil servants of the kind who create NGOs are constantly crossing the highly porous line between the social and the political. Allies, even supporters, of protest movements, they are simultaneously members of the Party and official bodies or even advisers to the Prince. They give talks in Party schools and lectures to leaders; at the same time they organise meetings with owners' associations, establish support structures and training sessions for migrants, advise activists in environmental organisations, expose the latest scandals and take part in collective mobilisations. Neither 'henchmen of the regime' nor 'dissidents', they play their own special role. They are far removed from the mythical figure of the Sartrean intellectual rebelling against power, but their actions are no less effective for that. They enjoy the discreet support of some leaders; they write reports for them; they defend 'social' positions in the newspapers. Once again possessing the aura of 'scholars' and experts, they are respected and listened to as long as they 'play the game', do not meddle in the political sphere, do not create a rival party or faction and do not encourage radicalism, and instead facilitate an understanding of problems, negotiations and dialogue with the discontented and the discovery of solutions. To adopt the formula employed by of one of them, 'since the political terrain is dangerous, it must be circumvented via the social'. By participating in the development of social movements, it is possible to force the political system, and especially those opposed to an increase in civil liberties, to change. They try to persuade national and local leaders that more freedom for people to object and defend their rights means more stability and that less freedom results in a proliferation of conflicts and an inability to 'manage' society effectively.[16]

To be effective and not experience too many difficulties, such internal critics must be protected. There is no critical research, condemnatory article, militant NGO, or civil liberties lawyer without the support, or at least benevolence, of people in high places. But power relations are complex and they must therefore act on guesswork and sometimes take risks. A provincial activist is received by a minister one day, and the next, when he returns home, local bureaucrats have him arrested to get him to stop demanding the closure of a factory. A journalist can denounce a scandal and, a few weeks later, find himself dismissed. A researcher may be authorised to write inflammatory texts and then receive a visit from the police inviting him to 'drink tea'—a polite way of indicating that he should back off and take a more cooperative stance.

Finally, the way that social science research is financed is itself indicative of the mix of genres. Two sources are available. On the one hand, public finance linked to the main issues confronting the authorities. On the other, finance from foreign foundations and international organisations, whose commissioning is based mainly on topics connected with modernisation theory. Hence, on the one hand, a heap of studies on migrants, the middle classes, consumption and management and, on the other, an enormous literature devoted to civil society, gender studies, and so forth. This provides little opportunity for basic research.

This intellectual and activist milieu represents a form of official opposition, which articulates questions and opposition that are kept secret within the apparatus. The controversies and struggles within it are fierce. It covers a large spectrum of political views. We find liberals who support a gradual retreat of the state as well as defenders of the 'new left', a constellation of figures who simultaneously defend national (even ultranationalist) ideas, the return of the state to the economy and the establishment of social policies. We also detect in it more open people, who reject any return to a form of socialism, but who believe that capitalism must be controlled and that wage-earners should be able to defend their interests under the auspices of an 'umpire' state. Such 'social democrats' are also the spearhead of the process of building a middle-class China.

Creating a Middle-Class China: A Source of Conflicts

Behind the seemingly consensual projects of the rugby ball, the olive, and of the setting up of a harmonious, prosperous and modern society, which we referred to earlier, in fact lies a whole series of political problems. China is prey to conflicts of interest and of imaginaries that challenge the modes of domination and 'classification' of Chinese society, and which will force the state into painful decisions in coming years—decisions that will displease some social category or other. The tax system is one of the most sensitive of these issues. Few people pay taxes, because a lot of income is informal. Capital gains on the stock market and the proceeds of corruption escape taxation. State enterprises pay nearly no tax on profit. Individual entrepreneurs or the bosses of private enterprises only declare part of their income and keep two sets of books. A more just direct tax system would include the benefits in kind, foreign travel and official cars enjoyed by technicians and civil servants. It would also challenge the social status of the elites and part of the middle classes and diminish the privileges of civil servants.

The abolition of the residence system, a recurrent issue in public policy, is another controversial subject. Everyone seems to believe that it represents the main systemic obstacle to the urban integration of migrant populations. By taking this decision, the state would enable new workers to benefit from public services in housing, professional training, and education. Employers hope it will lead to a homogenisation of the workforce, with urban employees losing their privileges, and hence to a reduction in labour costs. In contrast, they do not look with much favour on the establishment of a social security system. As for the old working class and the urban poor, they do not welcome the settlement of a population that is a potential rival in terms of social programmes and the labour market.

The 'deprived' have no voice of their own; others speak for them. Everyone seems to want 'to give peasants their chance' and demand measures in favour of the entry of peasants' children into university. But at whose expense? The urban residents who monopolise the channels of access to skilled work? Many would prefer a gradual transition, after which the 'best' immigrant children would join the ranks of town-dwellers and enjoy their privileges.

How is social protection to be extended? By improving the situation of urban residents, present or future (that is, migrants), or by ensuring the peasants a minimum? Who is to take responsibility for financing this protection? The central state or the local authorities? Employers? Employees? What will the impact on labour costs be? What compensation will the middle classes be offered for benefits conceded to those at the bottom of the scale, given that some of them believe poor people and peasants do not stand on their own two feet in the first place?

Identities and Nation

We cannot conclude this overview of political problems without broaching the issue of nationalism. Not only because it causes the spilling of much ink and fuels every kind of fear, from outsourcing to the invasion of Africa via the power of Chinese multinationals or the untold requirements of the economy in raw materials. But also because it represents a veritable moral reference point. The desire to see China restored to a certain greatness, and the emergence of a sense of pride at the Chinese nation's accomplishments, whether in the economic, social or cultural sphere, are very widely shared among Chinese citizens. One can be a homosexual activist, an exploited migrant, a trendy student, or critical intellectual, and oppose American imperialism, protest against 'French arrogance' during the Olympic torch relay in Paris, and participate in the various boycott movements that periodically run through society. Dissidents are not the last to assert that a democratic government will have to continue to demand the unconditional return of Taiwan to the national fold and to retain Tibet within the country's borders.

All this can only be explained by the place occupied by national 'memory' in the contemporary imaginary:[17] the memory of past Chinese greatness and the memory of the humiliation of foreign 'conquest' and Japanese invasion. This is more than just a propaganda effect—the whole world recognises the great age and historic glory of Chinese civilisation. Nevertheless, the decisive element in explaining the power of nationalism is a product of something universally acknowledged: apart from the socialism of the early 1950s, no other regime has succeeded in restoring power and a prominent place in the world to China and dignity to the Chinese population. In other words, China is living through a period of national self-assertion fairly similar to what Europe experienced in the nineteenth and twentieth centuries. The fate of individuals and social groups seems to be bound up with the national destiny: 'for me to succeed, China must succeed'. As long as the Party ensures the continuation of the country's rise to power, it will remain legitimate.

Even so, like any national identity, 'Chineseness' is full of contradictions. What is the basis of the nation? Culture? But how can one lump together in the same basket peasants, city-dwellers, the rich, the poor, northerners, southerners, the Han, and the national minorities? What to make of inhabitants of Hong Kong, the Taiwanese, or the overseas Chinese who no longer have Chinese nationality and, in some cases, have not had it for a long time? Blood—that is, membership of the Han ethnicity? But then how do we avoid a racial conception of the nation and regard members of national minorities as Chinese? How are those of 'mixed blood' to be classified? On the other hand, let us remember that identities, multiple by nature, are still more so today. Paradoxically, anyone who wants to help strengthen the Chinese nation must diversify affiliations and thus disassociate themselves from 'authenticity'. China's power does not lie in Daoist or Confucian masters, or the historians of the Han, but Harvard or Sciences-Po graduates, directors of large enterprises, cinema stars. The signs of a 'return' to tradition are undoubtedly legion. We witness the re-emergence of

Confucian schools and commentaries on the old philosophers are publishing successes. But all this is to help give China a greater role in the world and not to assert a different world-view or retreat to one's own 'values'. When people send their children to traditional schools, it is not to make them hermits or sages, but to teach them to learn and hence succeed more easily. We are still waiting for the emergence of a proper Chinese conception of the world.

Chinese nationalism is therefore neither a resurgence of the past, nor a desire for reversion to some Chinese essence. It is a practical formula enabling the Chinese to be modern—that is, to have roots, to produce a contemporary Chinese imaginary without abandoning the opportunities that present themselves. It is often a defensive formula, because, despite compliance with the global order—learning English and American education, the practice and idiom of international experts, cultural hybridisation—it makes it possible to assert one's specificity. Thanks to nationalist declarations, people can benefit individually from China's power—in terms of study grants, job opportunities, prestige, and various kinds of trading—while not being a 'traitor'. In China, the most nationalistic are often graduates of foreign universities, handle languages with skill, and sometimes have a foreign passport or at least a green card. Most Chinese film stars make a point of nationalism while being in possession of a foreign passport.

The rejection of electoral representation also makes it necessary to give the national reference an ahistorical and asocial form. As was evident during the Olympic ceremonies, or during the sixtieth anniversary of the People's Republic, the Chinese nation is as if outside time, because it brings together the whole history of China, including the thirty years of Maoism. To disown this heritage would be not only to disavow the actions of most of the leaders who implemented the reforms, but also to

131

be incapable of justifying the single Party any longer. It was the Party that made successful reform possible and the mistakes of the pre-reform years can only be attributed to the errant ways of leaders, not the Party itself. Preserving Mao as a tutelary power makes it possible to keep alive the historical mission of the CCP, which was to reawaken the country. The great importance still accorded the army refers to the same phenomenon. It is the symbol of necessary sacrifice for the nation. Omnipresent during major catastrophes, such as the avalanches in southern China in winter 2008 or after the earthquake in Sichuan in spring 2008, it also fills the museums more or less directly devoted to national liberation or reconstruction.

Conservative Democracy

The political question is therefore marked out by two horizons: on the one hand, 'democratisation', including in the long run the establishment of an electoral system, as deemed inevitable by all; on the other, fear of disorder that could endanger the rebirth of the Chinese state/nation. This is not the fear of a power at bay from a society that is emancipating itself, and whose clamour is increasingly difficult to contain. It runs through all social groups. We are therefore not dealing with the emergence of a civil society nibbling away at political power, but a mutual construction of increasingly inter-twined powerful forces. Social interests require channels of expression and need to influence the political decision-making process more directly. The state is establishing procedures of social regulation and professionalising its activity. But everyone fears the consequences of this dynamic and is asking questions. Will press freedom result in the stranglehold of a few major economic groups or hidden forces over public opinion? What are the limits of freedom of expression faced with disinformation, calumnies and rumours? Might not freedom to protest lead to disorder, interminable demands, neglect of the highest interests of the nation and society? Might not elections result in a republic of mediocrities or government paralysis at a time when instability and unpredictability should lead to a strengthening of state power? Might not liberalisation lead to a weakening of the capacity of the Chinese state for action.

Nothing very original, then, when it comes to the history of political change. Once the principle of the representation of social interests has been adopted, formulas that respect it without resulting in chaos will need to be found. In the case of China, this fear of chaos is the result of three factors. First of all, the terrible disruption of the Cultural Revolution, which, still profoundly marking the ruling generation (born in the 1940s and the 1950s), invests social order with every kind of virtue. Next, the forms of social habitus acquired in the past and propagated today in the new generation by parents. People like monitored residences, protected spaces, and settled lives. Thirdly, and finally, the improvement in the quality of life of a very great majority of the population, and rapid cultural changes, result in appreciation of the regime's achievements, while introducing new uncertainties—the need to save a sizeable sum to buy a flat, to pay for medical care, to send one's offspring abroad.

The paradox is that the possibility of elections is deemed 'disruptive' because of the undue solemnity with which representative democracy is treated. In China as all over the world, it is hard for most people not to regard democratisation in the same way as a religious phenomenon, where conversion, beliefs and revelation play a major role. The essence of democracy seems to precede its existence. Like the population, the state believes that citizens precede universal suffrage. Yet history demonstrates the reverse: it is the practice of universal suffrage that made the elector. In the major democracies, manipulation of the electoral register, collective voting, the purchase of polling cards, the stuffing of ballot boxes, and so on were long the rule rather than the exception—a rule generally favouring notables and the powerful. Research on village elections in China tends to show that people are generally not interested in elections because they do not change a lot, but this has been the case for decades in Europe.

In some government circles, people are aware of this because Party schools organize conferences on single-party experiences in bureaucratic regimes or on two-party systems. The objective is to find a system that could be formally democratic, without being the result of political confrontations between different interests and imaginaries. In other words, the democratization of institutions seems to be perceived as a technical problem, contributing to depoliticize political change. Nevertheless, all this is regarded as too complicated, too premature in so vast and diverse a country undergoing such a rapid pace of change. It is necessary to wait for the Chinese to become citizens—educated, politically conscious, and resolved to defend their interests and privilege the general and national interest. The aim is to create 'honest folk', of which homeowners are the archetype, before entrusting them with the reins of government.

Once the possibility of elections in the short term has been excluded, the debate becomes more complex. It is a question of finding a way of representing interests without an institutionalised formula. In local and national assemblies, all social milieus are represented: peasants, workers obviously, but also intellectuals, businessmen, and finally migrants. But it is the Party that continues to decide who can represent what. How could this practice withstand a serious economic crisis?

CONCLUSION

The perplexity of observers in the face of the astonishing changes undergone by China over the last thirty years or more stems from a methodological problem. Most of them seek to identify a substance, a nature, an absolute norm that would make it possible to explain everything rationally. Sometimes this involves a cultural determinism that supposedly runs through the whole social body. Sometimes it is a teleological logic, which seeks to characterise each stage on the basis of a final outcome that is posited *a priori*. Accordingly, inconsistencies in policy, behaviour and representations are perceived as deriving from poorly conducted, or poorly received, *transitions*. Ultimately, resistance to change will prove temporary and the final outcome will correspond to what theories of modernisation had postulated from the outset.

Once this mythology has been discarded, we can only affirm the normality of China. Not in the sense that it complies with a transcendent *norm*. Actually, Chinese society does not present mysterious features that cannot be grasped without recourse to something located outside it. In reality, the issues facing China are common ones. Its evolution closely aligns it with the condition experienced by other societies—and this for a very simple reason. In China, as elsewhere, it is supposed that there is a direction to history; that there is a certain convergence. But it is one thing to believe that an imaginary of modernisation exists and quite another to believe that reality is immediately, inherently, transcendentally driven by a modernising path—a road which it is impossible to exit. The difference between the two is that the imaginary of modernisation is incapable of avoiding the contradictions, impasses and paradoxes of the modernising process, because its performative effect encounters constant limits. It can ignore them, but the social sciences and, in particular, a critical use of their methods can expose them. Consequently, if the issues are common, the answers are not or, at any rate, not always. The imaginary of modernisation comes into conflict with other imaginaries. Accordingly interests are divergent; memories are multiple. This gives the way that Chinese society poses problems its own particular flavour.

Elements of Genealogy

What is the major problematic of Chinese society today? It is the emergence of a stratification based on the existence of a numerous 'middle class', which is supposed to rely on merit as the sole source of social success. While everyone is agreed in thinking that it is much too soon to establish a representative democracy, a broad consensus exists that the interests of different social groups must be better represented and better protected—in a word, better harmonised. Certainly, not all voices are equivalent. Naturally, those who are educated, people of 'quality' (*suzhi*), must be more influential. But vulnerable groups also deserve to have their opinions taken into account and their rights guaranteed, if only indirectly, via spokespersons or by co-opting some of their members. That is how we should interpret the announcement of the 'election' of several migrant workers as deputies to the eleventh National People's Congress (NPC) in 2008 and the 5.18 per cent increase in the number of migrants and peasants in the twelfth NPC in 2013 (a total of 401 representatives, or 13.42 per cent of the total number of deputies).

Meritocracy assumes adopting social policies that mitigate the most flagrant social disadvantages. Various programmes encourage the development of education in the countryside; health insurance funds are being created in rural areas; a minimum income has been established; a system of national insurance covers the totality of the contracted urban labour force. In China as elsewhere, it is universally known that all these measures are insufficient to give everyone equal opportunities, but they are regarded as conducive to a certain social justice.

This problematic is the product of a dual, convergent dynamic: a dynamic re-legitimating of the dominant class around 'modest prosperity' for all amid social stability; and a dynamic of upward mobility—albeit highly inegalitarian—for some social groups. This dual dynamic results in the 'Western model' being accorded a prominent role in the political imaginary. Contrary to the arguments of many Chinese and Western analysts, the general trend of Chinese society is closer to what we can call the Western trajectory than to a hypothetical Chinese model of society and very far from the modernization theory predictions. Social stratification must assume the shape of an olive because developed societies are supposed to have demonstrated that such is the ideal form for stimulating prosperity and maintaining social order. Similarly, reservations about the introduction of a system of representative democracy recall European societies in the nineteenth century and the first half of the twentieth century, which, regardless of social milieu, looked on universal suffrage with a generally hostile, anxious or sceptical eye. It took time and special circumstances to persuade one and all of its advantages. Finally, 'the rise of the middle classes', the issues of migration and urban integration, the adoption of social policies, and the invention of new traditions[1] are familiar themes to historians of the development of capitalism.

Why such a problematic in China at the start of the third millennium? Because the 1990s were marked by a radical questioning of Chinese society. The circumstances, like the habitus, of the Thermidorian elites compelled them to respond to this crisis. Can the Communist Party abandon the 'people', become completely 'capitalist', therewith risking the erosion of its power? Were not instability, poverty and foreign domination the gravediggers of the imperial regime and the Guomindang? The Party has therefore had to renew itself—renew its techniques of government, its personnel and its discourse.

In its turn, 1990s China, which witnessed the painful entry of much of the population into the capitalist labour system, and the commodification of capital, was responding to the crisis of the late 1980s, which culminated in the Tiananmen Square events. It was responding to a tense period for a society that had not left socialism behind and not really embarked on capitalism—a society already hungry for consumption and experience, but which wished to preserve its established rights; a society that was already being promised a great deal, but which did not have much and which did not want to lose anything. This period was fascinating because it was situated between two paradigms. For that very reason, however, it contained political dangers.

All is Well

This rapid genealogical glance might lead us to conclude that the reformist regime has been a 'success'. It enjoys wide popular support and its national leaders possess an undoubted aura. Naturally, support does not mean submissiveness. Criticisms pour forth from every quarter—criticism of corruption, injustices, inequalities, and so on. People want more freedom and opportunities. But the policies are deemed positive and the trends reckoned to be 'going in the right direction'. Ultimately, when it comes to the reforms, few really have anything to complain about—neither migrants, who are exploited but who are upwardly mobile nevertheless; nor workers, who have 'found another job' or seen their children become modern Chinese and 'moderately prosperous'; nor cadres, who have maintained and often improved their position; nor intellectuals, whose material comfort is combined with fairly extensive freedom of speech. Only peasants in remote regions external to this dynamic (but who is bothered about them?), and a small fringe of the urban population (about whom there are slight concerns), might think that they have gained nothing from the changes.

The reformist regime is the only one that has succeeded in what many have attempted: making the Chinese prosperous and China powerful. And people are grateful to it for that. So much so that even veterans of the democracy movements sometimes bitterly confide that, ultimately, had the Tiananmen movement prevailed, 'we wouldn't be where we are', but doubtless 'on a par with Russia'.

All this prompts us too to award a few laurels to the Chinese Thermidorian elites. Is not the Chinese 'miracle' attributable to the mix of revolutionary spirit and iron fist, lack of scruples and social concern, rapacity and fear of disorder—in short, the habitus of the last generation of 'historical Communists' and the generation of their children? Is the Chinese Thermidor a seamless transition to modernity?

However, this is to forget that explanations 'from above' are somewhat limited. The elites can 'construct' all they like; what ultimately 'takes shape' is often very different.[2] It is first necessary to take account of the habitus of other social strata—in particular, the urban strata who since 1949 have shared certain common values with the elites. The intimacy between workers and cadres, who formed part of the same world, has generated a common habitus, particularly in the way of valuing security and personal relations. There is nothing cultural or 'structural' about this. It stems from a shared experience—the totalitarian cellularisation of society in the village and work unit, which made personal relations an essential resource for living and surviving.

At a time of triumphant capitalism, what could be more natural than social capital becoming a factor of change and reduction in tension? It is a tool of domination and social success.[3] Without reliance on personal relations, there is no economic growth. Without the possibility of relying on parents, friends, classmates, colleagues, or teachers, there is no possibility of surviving, finding a good job or grant, investing capital, or obtaining the authorisation required to do business. It is a tool of social success, but also of solidarity. How many additional pensioners would fall into poverty without the support of their children? How many additional young graduates frustrated by uninteresting work, or the impossibility of opening a business, would there be in the absence of family support? How many workers would still be unemployed without a helping hand from a better-off colleague? In the end, without this factor, the sum of such discontents would doubtless have deprived the regime of any popular support and resulted in a major social crisis.

Finally, economic growth is a result of the reforms, but it is also a condition of their continuation, because it ensures stability. The rulers' actions have helped maintain social order without hobbling initiative: by associating civil servants with the benefits of the reforms; by eliminating the most retrograde and corrupt among them; by professionalising government; by changing modes of social control, and so forth. Nevertheless,

China's advantages have been decisive. China's population has been, and remains, a magnet for businessmen in search of cheap, plentiful, disciplined and relatively educated labour, and for those hungry for new outlets in a world where new frontiers for the consumer society are becoming scarce. In all these respects, China is unique. It is equally unique in its political power—its permanent seat on the UN Security Council, its atomic weapons—and its age-old cultural prestige. China is a past master in the art of infuriating and inspiring fear, but also in seducing. It knows how to use its symbolic capital, as is demonstrated by the success of Confucius Institutes the world over. All these advantages have been transformed into factors of economic growth and improved living standards.

Society is pursuing its dream of continual progress. Increasingly, the Chinese are 'individuals' who, while being preoccupied with themselves, voluntarily abide by the social norms created by communication, as generalised by everyday interactions, the media, associations, leisure, public policies and so on.[4] Politics continues to come down to 'household' affairs,[5] and the state is concerned with 'governing' the country in every detail: health, security, income, and so forth.[6] People are concerned with their personal development, while scrupulously assimilating the social codes of 'modernity'. They are increasingly striving to translate the new principles into reality: law instead of arbitrariness, social equity in place of equality, respect for social protest and the representation of interests, rather than repression and dictatorship. In short, Chinese society is modernising.

Modernisation is Not a Gala Dinner

However, if optimism about the country's stability seems to prevail in China and throughout the world, let us not forget

141

that, once extricated from its evolutionist mythology, modernisation is predominantly a matter of conflicts, contradictions, blood and tears. Above all, let us not forget that it is not some end of history. The prevailing optimism has certainly been further strengthened by the discomfiture of those who announced that the financial crisis would result in China's ruin. The twenty million registered unemployed migrants have disappeared or, at all events, have not taken to the streets; the graduates without a job are suffering in silence for now; growth is still strong and business is thriving. Growth has slowed since 2011, but still remains substantial.

Nevertheless, there is no lack of uncertainty—in the first instance, because continuing growth is an absolute necessity. It is the only way to satisfy the population's needs, which are themselves growing. The Chinese believe that an increase in living standards is something due to them; that an improvement in the quality of life over generations goes without saying; that it is only normal that tomorrow should be better than today. Growth has become a way of life. The children of migrants born in towns are not content with a significant but limited increase in their living standards. They want to have the same prospects as their urban contemporaries. In their turn, the latter want more than their parents. But how is growth to be maintained in a situation of external orientation and in the framework of such an unstable world economy? How is growth to be maintained while making the transition to an economy propelled by domestic demand and geared to the production of goods with higher value-added? Can China 'climb higher' without undergoing a difficult conversion phase?

However that may be, the pursuit of modernisation and growth through domestic demand inevitably leads to political conflicts. While the current middle class is favourable in principle to meritocracy, it is seeking to construct a society in its image, with its districts, lifestyle and criteria of social success, which distinguish it from the run-of-the-mill. It finds it difficult to accept neighbours who do not resemble it. It also finds it difficult to accept its signs of distinction—education and good manners—being democratised. Yet second- or third-generation migrants, born in the town or city, will not accept the status of second-class citizens as readily as their parents did. As for urban residents in difficulties, who are increasingly relegated to sub-urban areas, will they be the 'white trash' of a Chinese-style 'inner-city phenomenon'?

In other words, the creation of a middle-class China is a process in which the class struggle will play a major role. Everyone wants to belong to it, but access to the middle class is for now fairly limited (probably 25 per cent of the population) and its extension will be determined by the adoption of policies to be handled with care. No doubt the next frontier of reforms is the integration of migrants and popular urban milieus. The adoption of a housing policy, a more just tax system, more extensive social security—such are the next challenges. Finances will have to be massively directed towards these areas. But it is naïve to think that legislation does not entail arbitrary decisions. To protect private property is to favour those who already have it; to make competitive exams fairer and improve the education of the popular classes is not to take account of the role that will be played, in all kinds of ways, by cultural capital; to accept certain forms of—standard—protest is to prevent those that do not have the resources required to make themselves heard; to co-opt representatives from popular milieus is to exclude some of them.

Furthermore, the weakness of mechanisms for redistributing wealth does not make it possible to reduce the disparities today. Local finances are more and more under the control of the central state but, at the same time, huge amounts of extrabudgetary money are in the hands of local bureaucrats. Everyone 'gets by' and Beijing plays the role of fire fighter when the social situation deteriorates. It is hard to see how a real system of protection could be established without a centralisation or, at least, a regionalisation of funds—something that will likewise challenge certain established advantages.

The current domain of social movements, which is supposed to channel actual or potential conflicts, eludes any institutionalisation. There are no representative procedures, mechanisms, or organizations to take charge of discontent. It is the protesters and the local authorities who shape patterns of conflict, who come up with ways of resolving them or, at any rate, alleviating them. But these modalities remain fluid, change with the situation and introduce a significant factor of uncertainty.

Now, as the central government seems more open to compromise than before, protesters disagree on the attitude to take towards the organs of the state. In Beijing, the homeowners' movement has split between those who consider it necessary to cooperate with institutions and those who refuse that evolution. For Han Dongfang, the most important labour activist and founder of the Hong Kong-based *China Labour Bulletin*, the 'new era of activism' has forced China's official trade union, the All-China Federation of Trade Unions [ACFTU], to re-examine its role and look for ways to become an organisation that really does represent workers' interests. The ACFTU having introduced initiatives designed to boost workers' pay through negotiations with factory managers and business federation leaders, Han Dongfang considers that the international trade union movement should engage with the ACFTU. In contrast, Tim Pringle, a former employee of the *China Labour Bulletin*, says that 'it is important not to underestimate the challenges' of cooperating with the ACFTU: 'Bureaucratic box-ticking is one, along with the more institutional constraint of collusion between government, employers and trade unions at all levels in the name of economic growth and development'.[7]

Conservatism and Representation

For all that, can we hear the rumble of revolt? The new middle classes are not revolutionary, but we have known this for a long time.[8] With their 'favourite strategy, which consists in denouncing the established order in the name of the very principles it proclaims, the petit bourgeois bear witness to their recognition of those principles'.[9] To strikes and demonstrations they prefer pedagogy, information and the association, 'a strictly serial grouping of individuals assembled solely by the same "cause"'.[10] The middle classes are therefore agents and supporters of modernisation. They often organise effectively to protect their environment or establish greater legality. But, at the same time, they are allies of the regime. They demand respect for the individual, but are attached to conformity to behavioural models (good manners, the diktat of fashion) that have nothing revolutionary about them. They want more security and stability, which is perfectly in tune with the Party Line.

For other social milieus, the issues are different. Do they want to go on being represented by intellectuals or civil servants? Or, in the event of a long economic crisis, a sudden downturn, a chance event, or because of the maintenance of checks on social mobility, are they going to decide to assert themselves autonomously? Will the development of social policy and the activity of NGOs succeed in reducing social tension? If there is social rebellion, what forms will it take? Ghettoisation? The creation of 'reshaped' trade unions or of independent associations? A military coup? Contrary to what the supporters of models—be they Chinese or Western—say, the future of China is still wide open.

NOTES

INTRODUCTION

1. Lucian Pye, *The Mandarin and the Cadre*, Ann Arbor: Center for Chinese Studies, 1988; M.M. Yang, *Gifts, Favors, and Banquets: The Art of Social Relationships in China*, Ithaca and London: Cornell University Press, 1994.
2. Samuel Huntington, *Political Order in Changing Societies*, New Haven and London: Yale University Press, 2006; Ronald Inglehart, *Modernization and Post-Modernization: Cultural, Economic and Political Change in 43 Countries*, Princeton: Princeton University Press, 1997.
3. Just one example to demonstrate the point: the huge number of books on China that have 'transition' and 'transitional' in their titles, whatever the discipline.
4. Here also the number of books using *zhuanxing* in their titles is considerable. Even more importantly the term is at the core of many social sciences research.
5. Jean-François Bayart, *The Illusion of Cultural Identity*, Chicago/London: University of Chicago Press/C. Hurst & Co, 2005.
6. Colin Leys, *The Rise and Fall of Development Theory*, Bloomington/Nairobi/Oxford: Indiana University Press/EAEP/James Currey, 2009.
7. See works dealing with historical sociology, for example Theda Skocpol (ed.), *Vision and Method in Historical Sociology*, Cambridge: Cambridge University Press, 1984.
8. Eric Hobsbawm and Terence Ranger (eds), *The Invention of Tradition*, Cambridge: Cambridge University Press, 1983.
9. Nearly all the intellectuals and activists supporting collective

actions I interviewed argue that the Chinese society is not developed enough to set up a system of representative democracy. What is at stake is establishing a system of control over political leaders.

10. Richard Swedberg and Mark Granovetter (eds), *The Sociology of Economic Life*, Boulder: Westview Press, 192.

11. Skocpol, *Vision and Method*.

12. Françoise Mengin and Jean-Louis Rocca (eds), *Politics in China: Moving Frontiers*, New York: Palgrave, 2005.

13. Norbert Elias, *The Society of Individuals*, trans. Edmund Jephcott, Oxford: Blackwell, 1991.

14. Not far from constructivist but also people who are dealing with the role of imaginaries and representations.

15. For example, we will not deal with the issue of national minorities. It is an important issue from the standpoint of international relations and the geo-strategic balance. Important, too, because ethnic membership is one of the elements that determines the status of individuals—it is recorded on identity cards, including those of 'Chinese' ethnicity (Han). But it is marginal as regards its role in the workings of Chinese society. Representing a mere 7 per cent of the total population, for the most part minorities live on the margins of the most heavily populated and economically most decisive provinces. In some cases, they are fully integrated into Chinese life, while in others they are totally cut off from it. In the main, they are arbitrary inventions by the Chinese government, keen to clarify a social space that it had found very difficult to delimit. The classificatory criteria vary. Thus, the 'Uighurs' scarcely felt themselves to be Uighurs prior to 1949. Almost no 'Manchurians' now speak the language of their ancestors and they no longer possess any cultural specificity. The 'Hui' are Chinese whose only essential feature is their religion. Conversely, the 'Hakka' (*kejia*), a group of Chinese deriving from old migrations, who possess a language, their own customs and a genuine sense of belonging, do not constitute a minority. Furthermore, in the framework defined by the state, rather like what was created by colonial powers in Africa, ethnic identity is infinitely complicated. Although attached to the same religion, albeit in different contexts, the Hui and the Uighurs do not care for one another. Some

ethnicities are allied with the Han against other minorities. Many 'minority' citizens stick with their specificity for the good pragmatic reason that it permits then to have two children. On account of this 'marginality' and diversity (Smith, 2007; Hillman, 2005), taking the ethnic dimension of Chinese society into account would have required extended treatment exceeding the narrow bounds of this book. The main thing is to try to understand the broad lines of the mechanics of Chinese society. This should not be seen as implying any contempt for 'non-Hans'.

1. HISTORICAL TRAJECTORY

1. See Jean-François Bayart, *The State in Africa: the Politics of the Belly*, London: Longman, 1993, *Global Subjects: A Political Critique of Globalization*, New York: Polity Press, 2008.
2. On Republican China (1911–49), see John K. Fairbank and Denis Twitchett (eds), *The Cambridge History of China, Vol. 12, Republican China, Part 1*, Cambridge: Cambridge University Press, 1983; John K. Fairbank and Albert Feuerwerker (eds), *The Cambridge History of China, Vol. 13, Republican China, Part 2*, Cambridge: Cambridge University Press, 1986; Rana Mitter, *Modern China: A Very Short History*, Oxford and New York: Oxford University Press, 2008; Jonathan D. Spence, *The Search for Modern China*, New York: Norton, 1999; Prasenjit Duara, *Culture, Power and the State: Rural North China 1900–1942*, Stanford: Stanford University Press, 1988.
3. Yves Chevrier, *La Chine moderne*, Paris: Presses Universitaires de France, 1997.
4. Yves Chevrier, 'L'empire distendu: esquisse du politique en Chine des Qing à Deng Xiaoping', in Jean-François Bayart (ed.), *La Greffe de l'État*, Paris: Karthala, 1996, pp. 262–395.
5. For an overall approach to socialist China, see Roderick MacFarquhar and John K. Fairbank (eds), *The Cambridge History of China*, volumes 14 and 15, Cambridge: Cambridge University Press, 1987 and 1991.
6. Simon Leys, *Chinese Shadows*, New York: The Viking Press, 1977, *The Chairman's New Clothes. Mao and the Cultural Revolution*, New York: Palgrave MacMillan, 1978; Hector Mandarès

et al (eds), *Révolution culturelle dans la Chine populaire. Anthologie de la presse des Gardes rouges, mai 1966–janvier 1968*, Paris: Union générale d'éditions, 1974. See also memories of red guards like Liang Heng, *Son of the Revolution*, New York: Vintage Books, 1983.

7. Jean Oi, *State and Peasant in Contemporary China: The Political Economy of Village Government*, Berkeley: University of California Press, 1989; Martin M. Whyte and William M. Parish, *Village and Family in Contemporary China*, Chicago: Chicago University Press, 1978, *Urban Life in Contemporary China*, Chicago: Chicago University Press, 1984; Andrew A. Walder, *Communist Neo-traditionalism: Work and Authority in Chinese Industry*, Berkeley, Los Angeles and London: University of California Press, 1986.

8. Walder, *Communist Neo-Traditionalist*; Whyte and Parish, *Village and Family in Contemporary China* and *Urban Life in Contemporary China*.

9. Merle Goldman, Timothy Cheek and Carol Lee Hamrin (eds), *China's Intellectuals and the State: in Search of a New Relationship*, Cambridge: Cambridge University Press, 1987.

10. Jean Pasqualini [Bao Ruowang] and Rudolph Chelminski, *Prisoner of Mao*, London: André Deutch, 1975.

11. Elizabeth Croll, *Chinese Women since Mao*, London: Third World Books, 1983; Liu Jieyu, *Gender and Work in Urban China: Women Workers of the Unlucky Generation*, London and New York: Routledge, 2007; Tang Xiaojing, *'Femmes au foyer', 'filles de fer' et retour au foyer. Genre et travail à Shanghai sur quatre générations, 1949–2007*, doctoral thesis in sociology, EHESS-ENS-ECNU, 2009.

11. Whyte and Parish, *Village and Family in Contemporary China* and *Urban Life in Contemporary China*; Jackie Sheehan, *Chinese Worker: A New History*, London and New York: Routledge, 1998.

13. Walder, *Communist Neo-Traditionalism*.

14. Leys, *Chinese Shadows*; Mandarès et al (eds), *Révol. cul. dans la Chine pop.*

15. Jasper Becker, *Hungry Ghosts: China's Secret Famine*, London: John Murray, 1996; John K. Fairbank, *The Great Chinese Revolution 1800–1985*, New York: Harper & Row, 1987.

2. THE LONG MARCH OF REFORMS

1. Fariba Adelkah, Jean-François Bayart and Olivier Roy, *Thermidor en Iran*, Brussels: Complexe, 1993; Jean-François Bayart, 'Le concept de situation thermidorienne: régimes néo-révolutionnaires et libéralisation économique', *Research in Question*, 24, March 2008, www.sciencespo.fr/ceri/sites/sciencespo.fr.ceri/files/qdr24.pdf

2. Hannah Arendt, *The Human Condition*, Chicago: Chicago University Press, 1999.

3. Bruce J. Dickson, *Red Capitalists in China: the Party, Private Entrepreneurs, and Prospects for Political Change*, Cambridge: Cambridge University Press, 2003; Jean C. Oi, *Rural China Takes Off: Institutional Foundations of Economic Reform*, Berkeley: University of California Press, 1999; David Wank, *Commodifying Communism: Business, Trust and Politics in a Chinese City*, Cambridge: Cambridge University Press, 2001.

4. Karl Polanyi, *The Great Transformation*, Boston: Beacon Press, 1944; Fernand Braudel, *La dynamique du capitalisme*, Paris: Arthaud, 1985.

5. Oi, *Rural China Takes Off*; Jackie Sheehan, *Chinese Worker: A New History*, London and New York: Routledge, 1998; Barry Naughton, *The Chinese Economy: Transitions, and Growth*, Cambridge and London: MIT Press, 2006.

6. Naughon, *The Chinese Economy*; Jean-Louis Rocca, *La condition chinoise. La mise au travail capitaliste à l'âge des réformes*, Paris: Karthala, 2006.

7. Ole Bruun, *Business and Bureaucracy: An Ethnography of Private Business Households in Contemporary China*, Berkeley: University of California Press, 1993.

8. Yves Chevrier, 'Micropolitics and the Factory Director Responsibility System, 1984–1987' in Deborah Davis and E. Vogel (eds), *Chinese Society on the Eve of Tiananmen: The Impact of Reform*, Cambridge: Harvard University Press, 1990, pp. 109–133.

9. Dickson, *Red Capitalists in China*; Margaret Pearson, *China New's Business Elite: The Political Consequences of Reform*, Berkeley: University of California Press, 1997.

10. Christopher C. Findlay, Andrew Watson and Harry Wu, *Rural*

Enterprises in China, Basingstoke/New York: MacMillan/St Martin's Press, 1994.

11. Ole Bruun, *Business and Bureaucracy*.

12. Lin Yimin, *Between Politics and Markets*, Cambridge: Cambridge University Press, 2001.

13. Jean-Louis Rocca (ed.), *La société chinoise vue par ses sociologues*, Paris: Presses de Sciences Po 2008; Aurore Merle and Zhang Lun, 'La Chine en transition: regards sociologiques', *Cahiers internationaux de sociologie*, vol. 122, 2007, pp. 5–168; Isabelle Thireau and Wang Hansheng, *Disputes au village chinois. Formes du juste et recompositions locales des espaces normatifs*, Paris: Editions de la MSH, 2001.

14. Among the most interesting books on the subject, see Zhang Lian, *The Tiananmen Papers*, London: Abacus, 2002; Zhao Dingxin, *The Power of Tiananmen: State-society Relations and the 1989 Beijing Student Movement*, Chicago: Chicago University Press, 2001.

15. In the sense employed by Arendt; see Arendt, *Human Condition*.

16. Françoise Mengin, *Fragments d'une guerre inachevée. Les entrepreneurs taiwanais et la partition de la China*, Paris: Karthala, 2013.

17. Benedict Anderson, *Imagined Communities: Reflections on the Origin and Spread of Nationalism*, London: Verso, 1991.

18. Polanyi, *The Great Transformation*.

19. Robert Castel, *From Manual Workers to Wage Laborers: Transformation of the Social Question*, New Brunswick, NJ: Transaction Publishers, 2003.

20. Rocca, *La condition chinoise*; William Hurst, *The Chinese Worker after Socialism*, Cambridge: Cambridge University Press, 2009.

21. Rocca, *La condition chinoise*; Hurst, *The Chinese Worker after Socialism*; Thomas Gold, William Hurst, Won Jaeyoun and Li Qiang (eds), *Laid-Off Workers in a Workers' State: Unemployment with Chinese Characteristics*, New York: Palgrave MacMillan, 2009.

22. Pearson, *China's New Business Elite*; Wank, *Commodifying Communism*; Dickson, *Red Capitalists in China*.

23. http://www.chinahrd.net/news/regional-news/2012/1212/182353.html

24. Sophie Song, 'Chinese College Graduates Cannot Secure Jobs: 28% Of Beijing's 2013 Graduates and 44% Of Shanghai's Have Found A Job', *International Business Times*, July 15, 2014, www.ibtimes.com/chinese-college-graduates-cannot-secure-jobs-28-beijings-2013-graduates-44-shanghais-have-found-job

25. http://edu.qq.com/a/20130609/013282.html

26. http://www.cnr.cn/gundong/201207/t20120726_510345563.shtml

27. Kam Wing Chan and Will Buckingham, 'Is China Abolishing the *Hukou* System?', *The China Quarterly*, 195, September 2008, pp. 582–606.

28. Li Jian and Niu Xiaohan, 'The New Middle Class(es) in Peking: A Case Study', *China Perspectives*, 45, January–February 2003, pp. 4–20.

29. Zhao Weihua, *Diwei yu xiaofei* [Status and consumption], Beijing: Shehui kexue wenxuan chubanshe, 2007.

3. A NEW SOCIETY

1. Rachel Murphy (ed.), *Labour Migration and Social Development in Contemporary China*, London and New York: Routledge, 2009.

2. Li Peilin, Li Qiang and Sun Liping, *Zhongguo shehui fenceng* [The Stratification of Chinese Society], Beijing: Shehui kexue wenxian chubanshe, 2004.

3. Lin Yi, *Cultural Exclusion in China: State Education, Social Mobility and Cultural Difference*, London and New York: Routledge, 2008; Amy Hanser, *Service Encounters: Class, Gender, and the Market For Social Distinction in Urban China*, Stanford: Stanford University Press, 2008; Carolyn L. Hsu, *Creating Market Socialism: How Ordinary People Are Shaping Class and Status in China*, Durham NC and London: Duke University Press, 2007.

4. Isabelle Thireau and Wang Hansheng, *Disputes au village chinois. Formes du juste et recompositions locales des espaces normatifs*, Paris: Editions de la MSH, 2001.

5. Lu Xueyi (ed.), *Dangdai zhongguo shehui jieceng yanjiu baogao* [Research Report on Social Strata in Contemporary China], Beijing: Shehui kexue wenxian chubanshe, 2002.

6. Cf. websites of the International Monetary Fund, the World Bank, the Asian Development Bank, and the United Nations Development Programme.

7. Li, Li and Sun, *Zhongguo shehui fenceng*; Lu Xueyi (ed.), *Dangdai zhongguo shehui jiegou* [The Social Structure in China Today], Beijing: Shehui kexue wenxian chubanshe, 2010; Lu Xueyi (ed.), *Dangdai zhongguo shehui jieceng yanjiu baogao*; Lu Xueyi (ed.), *Dangdai zhongguo shehui liudong* [Social Mobility in Contemporary China], Beijing: Shehui kexue wenxian chubanshe, 2004; Zhao Weihua, *Diwei yu xiaofei* [Status and consumption], Beijing: Shehui kexue wenxuan chubanshe, 2007.

8. Zhou Xiaohong, 'Chinese Middle Class: Reality or Illusion?' in Christophe Jaffrelot and Peter Van der Veer (eds), *Patterns of Middle Class and Consumption in India and China*, New Delhi: Sage, 2008, pp. 110–126.

9. Jean-Louis Rocca, 'Power of Knowledge: The Imaginary Formation of the Chinese Middle Class Stratum in an Era of Reform' in Jaffrelot and Van Der Veer (eds), *Patterns of Middle Class Consumption*; Jean-Louis Rocca, 'Homeowners' Movements: Narratives on the Political Behaviours of the Middle Class' in David Goodman and Chen Minglu, *Middle Class China: Identity and Behaviour*, Northampton: Edward Elgar, 2013, pp. 110–134.

10. Rocca, 'Homeowners' movements'; Zhang Li, *In Search of Paradise: Middle-Class Living in a Chinese Metropolis*, Ithaca, NY and London: Cornell University Press, 2010.

4. A SOCIETY OF INDIVIDUALS IN A TIME OF REFORMS

1. Norbert Elias, *The Society of Individuals*, trans. Edmund Jephcott, Oxford: Blackwell, 1991.

2. Deborah Davis (ed.), *Urban Spaces in Contemporary China: The Potential for Autonomy and Community in Post-Mao China*, Washington, DC/Cambridge: Woodrow Wilson Center Press/Cambridge University Press, 1995; Deborah Davis (ed.), *The Consumer Revolution in Urban China*, Berkeley, Los Angeles and London: University of California Press, 2000.

3. See Michel Foucault, *The History of Sexuality, Vol. 1: The Will to Knowledge, Vol. 2 The Use of Pleasure, Vol. 3, The Care of Self*, London: Penguin, 1979, 1992, 1984.

4. Amy Hanser, *Service Encounters: Class, Gender, and the Market For Social Distinction in Urban China*, Stanford: Stanford University Press, 2008; Jean-Louis Rocca, 'Homeowners' Movements: Narratives on the Political Behaviours of the Middle Class' in David Goodman and Chen Minglu, *Middle Class China: Identity and Behaviour*, Northampton: Edward Elgar, 2013, pp. 110–134; Zhang Li, *In Search of Paradise: Middle-Class Living in a Chinese Metropolis*, Ithaca, NY and London: Cornell University Press, 2010.

5. Lisa Rofel, *Desiring China: Experiments in Neoliberalism, Sexuality, and Public Culture*, Durham, NC, and London: Duke University Press, 2009.

5. THE POLITICAL PUZZLE

1. Andrew Nathan, 'Authoritarian Resilience', *Journal Democracy*, vol. 14, no. 1, January 2003, pp. 6–17.

2. Michel Foucault, *The History of Sexuality, Vol. 1: The Will to Knowledge*, London: Penguin, 1979.

3. Françoise Mengin, *Cyber China: Reshaping National Identities in the Age of Information*, New York: Palgrave, 2004.

4. Michel Offerlé, *Un homme, une voix? Histoire du suffrage universel*, Paris: Gallimard, 1993.

5. Jean-Louis Rocca, *La condition chinoise. La mise au travail capitaliste à l'âge des réformes (1978–2004)*, Paris: Karthala, 2006.

6. Jean Oi and Zhao Shukai, 'Direct Township Elections', in E. Perry and H. Goldman, *Grassroots Political Reform in Contemporary China*, Cambridge: Harvard University Press, 2007.

7. Randall Peerenboom, *China's Long March toward Rule of Law*, Cambridge: Cambridge University Press, 2002.

8. Thomas Gold, Doug Guthrie and David Wank (eds), *Social Connections in China: Institutions, Culture, and the Changing Nature of Guanxi*, Cambridge: Cambridge University Press, 2002.

9. Jean-Louis Rocca, 'Homeowners' Movements: Narratives on the Political Behaviours of the Middle Class' in David Goodman and Chen Minglu, *Middle Class China: Identity and Behaviour*, Northampton: Edward Elgar, 2013, pp. 110–134.

10. Foucault, *The History of Sexuality*.

11. Rocca, 'Homeowners' Movements'.

12. Shen Jie, *Labour Disputes and their Resolution in China*, Oxford: Chandos Publishing, 2007, p. 73.

13. See 'China's Workers Demand a Better Trade Union', *China Labour Bulletin*, 22 March, 2013, http://clb.org.hk/en/content/china's-workers-demand-better-trade-union

14. Social management is a slogan that appeared at the end of the 1980s beginning of the 1990s. Broadly speaking, we can define social management as an array of new policies, new mechanisms, new ways which aim at preventing social problems and social conflicts in order to reduce social unrest and protecting the stability of the society. That concerns a huge range of tools: social services, workplace safety, dispute resolution, and police. A specific organ, the Central Comprehensive management Commission (*Zhongyang shehui guanli zonghe zhili weiyuanhui*), is in charge of setting major policies of social management.

15. On Chinese NGOs, see Lu Yiyi, *Non-Governmental Organizations in China*, Abingdon UK: Routledge, 2009.

16. Guo Yuhua, Jing Jun, Shen Yuan and Sun Liping, *Yiliyi biaoda zhiduhua shixian shehui de changzhi jiuan* [Relying on an institutionalisation of interest expression for bringing about a long period of political stability], Tsinghua University Research Group on Social Development, 2010.

17. Benedict Anderson, *Imagined Communities. Reflections on the Origin and Spread of Nationalism*, London: Verso, 1991.

CONCLUSION

1. Eric Hobsbawn and Terence Ranger (eds), *The Invention of Tradition*, Cambridge: Cambridge University Press, 1992.

2. Bruce Berman and John Lonsdale, *Unhappy Valley. Conflict in Kenya and Africa*, vol. 1, London: James Currey, 1992.

3. Thomas Gold, Doug Guthrie, David Wank (eds), *Social Connections in China: Institutions, Culture, and the Changing Nature of Guanxi*, Cambridge: Cambridge University Press, 2002.

4. Norbert Elias, *The Society of Individuals*, trans. Edmund Jephcott, Oxford: Blackwell, 1991.

5. Hannah Arendt, *The Human Condition*, Chicago: Chicago University Press, 1999.
6. Michel Foucault, *The History of Sexuality, Vol. 1: The Will to Knowledge*, London: Penguin, 1979.
7. Han Dongfang 'The Guardian: China's Main Union is Yet to Earn its Job', *China Labour Bulletin*, 27 June 2011 http://www.clb.org.hk/en/content/guardian-chinas-main-union-yet-earn-its-job
8. C. Wright Mills, *White Collar: The American Middle Class*, Oxford: Oxford University Press, 1951; Pierre Bourdieu, *Distinction: A Social Critique of the Judgement of Taste*, Abingdon: Routledge, 1984; Luc Boltanski, *The Making of a Class: Cadres in French Society*, Cambridge: Cambridge University Press, 1983.
9. Bourdieu, *Distinction*, p. 456.
10. *Ibid*, p. 457.

SELECT BIBLIOGRAPHY

Adelkah, Fariba, Jean-François Bayart and Olivier Roy (1993), *Thermidor en Iran*, Brussels: Complexe.

Anderson, Benedict (1991), *Imagined Communities. Reflections on the Origin and Spread of Nationalism*, London: Verso.

Arendt, Hannah (1999), *The Human Condition*, Chicago and London: University of Chicago Press.

Bai, Limin (2001), 'Children's Performance, Parental Expectations and China's Education in the 1990s', *Asian Profile*, vol. 29, no. 3, pp. 185–207.

Bandurski, David and Martin Hala (eds) (2010), *Investigative Journalism in China*, Seattle: University of Washington Press.

Bayart, Jean-François (2005), *The Illusion of Cultural Identity*, Chicago/London: University of Chicago Press/C. Hurst & Co.

—— (1993), *The State in Africa: the Politics of the Belly*, London: Longman.

—— (2008), *Global Subjects: A Political Critique of Globalization*, New York: Polity Press.

—— (2008), 'Le concept de situation thermidorienne: régimes néo-révolutionnaires et libéralisation économique', *Research in Question*, no. 24, March 2008, www.sciencespo.fr/ceri/sites/sciencespo.fr.ceri/files/qdr24.pdf

Becker, Jasper (1996), *Hungry Ghosts: China's Secret Famine*, London: John Murray.

Berman, Bruce and John Lonsdale (1992), *Unhappy Valley: Conflict in Kenya and Africa*, Vol. 1, London: James Currey.

Bernstein, T.P. and Lü Xiabo (2003), *Taxation without Representation in Contemporary China*, Cambridge: Cambridge University Press.

159

Boltanski, Luc (1983), *The Making of a Class: Cadres in French Society*, Cambridge: Cambridge University Press.

Bonnin, Michel (2004), *Génération perdue. Le mouvement d'envoi des jeunes instruits à la campagne en Chine, 1968–1980*, Paris: Éditions de l'EHESS.

Bourdieu, Pierre (1984), *Distinction: A Social Critique of the Judgement of Taste*, trans. Richard Nice, Abingdon: Routledge.

Braudel, Fernand (1985), *La dynamique du capitalisme*, Paris: Arthaud.

Bruun, Ole (1993), *Business and Bureaucracy: An Ethnography of Private Business Households in Contemporary China*, Berkeley: University of California Press.

Cai, Yongshu (2010), *Collective Resistance in China: Why Popular Protests Succeed or Fail*, Stanford CA: Stanford University Press.

Castel, Robert (2002), *From Manual Workers to Wage Laborers: Transformation of the Social Question*, trans. Richard Boyd, New Brunswick: Transaction Publishers.

Chan, Kam Wing and Will Buckingham (2007), 'Is China Abolishing the *Hukou* System?', *The China Quarterly*, 195, September, pp. 582–606.

Chen, Xi (2012), *Social Protest and Contentious Authoritarianism in China*, Cambridge and New York: Cambridge University Press.

Chevrier, Yves (1990), 'Micropolitics and the Factory Director Responsibility System, 1984–1987', in D. Davis and E. Vogel (eds), *Chinese Society on the Eve of Tiananmen: The Impact of Reform*, Cambridge (MA): Harvard University Press, pp. 109–33.

—— (1996), 'L'empire distendu: esquisse du politique en Chine des Qing à Deng Xiaoping', in J.-F. Bayart (ed.), *La Greffe de l'État*, Paris: Karthala, pp. 262–395.

—— (1997), *La Chine moderne*, Paris: Presses Universitaires de France.

'China's Workers Demand a Better Trade Union', *China Labour Bulletin*, 22 March, 2013 http://clb.org.hk/en/content/china's-workers-demand-better-trade-union

Croll, Elizabeth (1983), *Chinese Women since Mao*, London: Third World Books.

Davis, Deborah (ed.) (1995), *Urban Spaces in Contemporary China: The Potential for Autonomy and Community in Post-Mao China*,

Washington, DC/Cambridge: Woodrow Wilson Center Press/ Cambridge University Press.

—— (ed.) (2000), *The Consumer Revolution in Urban China*, Berkeley, Los Angeles and London: University of California Press.

—— (2003), 'From Welfare Benefit to Capitalized Asset', in R. Forrest and J. Lee (eds), *Housing and Social Change: East-West Perspectives*, New York: Routledge, pp. 83–196.

Dickson, Bruce (2003), *Red Capitalists in China: The Party, Private Entrepreneurs, and Prospects for Political Change*, Cambridge: Cambridge University Press.

Domenach, Jean-Luc (1992), *Chine: l'archipel oublié*, Paris: Fayard.

Duara, Prasenjit (1988), *Culture, Power and the State: Rural North China 1900–1942*, Stanford: Stanford University Press.

Elias, Norbert (1991), *The Society of Individuals*, trans. Edmund Jephcott, Oxford: Blackwell.

—— (2000), *The Civilizing Process*, trans. Edmund Jephcott, Oxford: Blackwell.

Fairbank, John K. (1987), *The Great Chinese Revolution 1800–1985*, New York: Harper & Row.

Fairbank, John K. and Denis Twitchett (eds) (1983), *The Cambridge History of China, Vol. 12, Republican China, Part 1*, Cambridge: Cambridge University Press.

Fairbank, John K. and Albert Feuerwerker (eds) (1986), *The Cambridge History of China, Vol. 13, Republican China, Part 2*, Cambridge: Cambridge University Press.

Findlay, Christopher, Andrew Watson and Harry Wu (eds) (1994), *Rural Enterprises in China*, New York: St. Martin's Press.

Fong, Vanessa L. (2012), *Paradise Redefined: Transnational Chinese Students and the Quest for Flexible Citizenship in the Developed World*, Stanford: Stanford University Press.

Foucault, Michel (1979), *History of Sexuality, Vol. 1, The Will to Knowledge*, trans. Robert Hurley, London: Penguin.

—— (1998), *History of Sexuality, Vol. 2, The Use of Pleasure*, trans. Robert Hurley, London: Penguin.

—— (1984), *History of Sexuality, Vol. 3, The Care of Self*, trans. Robert Hurley London: Penguin.

Frazier, Mark W. (2002), *The Making of the Chinese Industrial Workplace: State, Revolution, and Labor Management*, Cambridge: Cambridge University Press.

———— (2004), 'China's Pension Reform and its Discontents', *China Journal*, no. 51, pp. 97–114.

Gold, Thomas, Dough Guthrie, and David Wank (eds) (2002), *Social Connections in China: Institutions, Culture, and the Changing Nature of the Guanxi*, Cambridge: Cambridge University Press.

Gold Thomas, William Hurst Jaeyoun Won and Li Qiang (eds) (2009), *Laid-Off Workers in a Workers' State: Unemployment with Chinese Characteristics*, New York: Palgrave/MacMillan.

Goldman, Merle, Timothy Cheek and Carol Lee Hamrin (eds) (1987), *China's Intellectuals and the State: in Search of a New Relationship*, Cambridge: Cambridge University Press.

Greenhalgh, Susan (2010), *Cultivating Global Citizens: Population in the Rise of China*, Cambridge MA: Harvard University Press.

Guillermaz, Jacques (1972), *A History of the Chinese Communist Party 1921–1949*, trans. Anne Destenay, London: Methuen.

———— (1976), *The Chinese Communist Party in Power 1949–1976*, trans. Anne Destenay, Boulder: Westview Press.

Guo, Yuhua, Jing Jun, Shen Yuan and Sun Liping (2010), *Yiliyi biaoda zhiduhua shixian shehui de changzhi jiuan* [Relying on an institutionalisation of interest expression for bringing about a long period of political stability], Tsinghua University Research Group on Social Development.

Han, Dongfang (2011) 'The Guardian: China's Main Union is Yet to Earn its Job', *China Labour Bulletin*, 27 June http://www.clb.org.hk/en/content/guardian-chinas-main-union-yet-earn-its-job

Hanser, Amy (2008), *Service Encounters: Class, Gender and the Market for Social Distinction in Urban China*, Stanford: Stanford University Press.

Hayhoe, Ruth (1996), *China's Universities 1895–1995: A Century of Cultural Conflict*, New York: Garland.

Hermet, Guy (1996), *Le Passage à la démocratie*, Paris: Presses de la FNSP.

Hershatter, Gail (2011), *The Gender of Memory: Rural Women and China's Collective Past*, Berkeley: University of California Press.

Hillman, Ben (2005), 'Monastic Politics and the Local State in China: Authority and Autonomy in an Ethnically Tibetan Prefecture', *China Journal*, no. 54, pp. 29–51.

Hood, Johanna (2011), *HIV/AIDS, Health and the Media in China*, London and New York: Routledge.

Hsu, Carolyn L. (2007), *Creating Market Socialism: How Ordinary People are Shaping Class and Status in China*, Durham, NC and London: Duke University Press.

Hobsbawm, Eric and Terence Ranger (eds) (1983), *The invention of Tradition*, Cambridge: Cambridge University Press.

Huntington, Samuel (2006), *Political Order in Changing Societies*, New Haven and London: Yale University Press.

Hurst, William (2009), *The Chinese Worker after Socialism*, Cambridge: Cambridge University Press.

Inglehart, Ronald (1997), *Modernization and Post-Modernization: Cultural, Economic and Political Change in 43 Countries*, Princeton: Princeton University Press.

Journal of Contemporary China (2009), special issue, no. 60.

Lee, Ching-Kwan (1998), *Gender and the South China Miracle: Two Worlds of Factory Women*, Berkeley, Los Angeles and London: University of California Press.

—— (2007), *Working in China: Ethnographies of Labor and Workplace Transformation*, London and New York: Routledge.

Leys, Colin (1996), *The Rise and Fall of Development Theory*, Bloomington/Nairobi/Oxford: Indiana University Press/EAEP/James Currey.

Leys, Simon (1977), *The Chairman's New Clothes*, trans. P. Goode, London: Allison & Busby.

—— (1978), *Chinese Shadows*, Harmondsworth: Penguin.

Li, Cheng (2008), *China's Changing Political Landscape*, Washington: Brookings Institution.

Li, Chunling (2003), 'Zhongguo dangdai zhongchan jieceng de goucheng ji bili' ['Structure and Size of the Middle Stratum in Contemporary China'], *Zhongguo renkou kexue*, no. 6, pp. 25–52.

Li, Jian and Niu Xioahuan (2003), 'The New Middle Class(es) in Peking: A Case Study', *China Perspectives*, no. 45, pp. 4–20.

Li, Peilin, Li Qiang and Sun Liping (2004), *Zhongguo shehui fenceng* [The Stratification of Chinese Society], Beijing: Shehui kexue wenxian chubanshe.

Liang, Heng (1983), *Son of the Revolution*, Vintage Books.

Lin, Jing and Zhang Yu (2006), 'Educational Expansion and Shortages in Secondary Schools in China: The Bottle Neck Syndrome', *Journal of Contemporary China*, vol. 15, no. 47, pp. 255–74.

Lin, Yi (2008), *Cultural Exclusion in China: State Education, Social Mobility and Cultural Difference*, London and New York: Routledge.

Lin, Yimin (2001), *Between Politics and Markets*, Cambridge: Cambridge University Press.

Liu, Jieyu (2007), *Gender and Work in Urban China: Women Workers of the Unlucky Generation*, London and New York: Routledge.

Lu, Caizhen (2012), *Poverty and Development in China: Alternative Approaches to Poverty Assessment*, London and New York, Routledge.

Lu, Xueyi (ed.) (2002), *Dangdai zhongguo shehui jieceng yanjiu baogao* [Research Report on Social Strata in Contemporary China], Beijing: Shehui kexue wenxian chubanshe.

—— (2004), *Dangdai zhongguo shehui liudong* [Social Mobility in Contemporary China], Beijing: Shehui kexue wenxian chubanshe.

—— (2010), *Dangdai zhongguo shehui jiegou* [The Social Structure in China Today], Beijing: Shehui kexue wenxian chubanshe.

Lu, Yiyi (2009), *Non-Governmental Organizations in China*, Abingdon, UK: Routledge.

Lü, Xiaobo and Elizabeth Perry (1997), *Danwei: The Changing Workplace in Historical and Comparative Perspective*, Armonk, NY, and London: M.E. Sharpe.

McConville, Mike (2011), *Criminal Justice in China: An Empirical Inquiry*, Cheltenham and Northampton, MA: Edward Elgar.

McFarquhar, Roderick and John K. Fairbank (eds) (1987), *The Cambridge History of China, Vol. 14: The People's Republic, Part 1: The Emergence of Revolutionary China, 1949–1965*, Cambridge: Cambridge University Press.

—— (1991) *The Cambridge History of China, Vol. 15 The People's Republic, Part 2: Revolutions within the Chinese revolution, 1966–1982*, Cambridge: Cambridge University Press.

Mandarès, H. et al (eds) (1974), *Révol. cul. dans la Chine pop. Anthologie de la presse des Gardes rouges, mai 1966–janvier 1968*, Paris: Union générale d'éditions.

Mengin, Françoise (2004), *Cyber China: Reshaping National Identities in the Age of Information*, New York: Palgrave.

—— (2015), *Fragments of an Unfinished War: Taiwanese Entrepreneurs and the Partition of China*, London: C. Hurst & Co.

Mengin, Françoise and Jean-Louis Rocca (2002), *Politics in China: Moving Frontiers*, New York: Palgrave.

Merle, Aurore, and Zhang Lun (2007), 'La Chine en transition: regards sociologiques', *Cahiers internationaux de sociologie*, vol. 122, pp. 5–168.

Mills, C. Wright (1951), *White Collar: The American Middle Class*, Oxford: Oxford University Press.

Mitter, Rana (2008), *Modern China: A Very Short History*, Oxford and New York: Oxford University Press.

Murphy, Rachel (2009), *Labour Migration and Social Development in China*, London: Routledge.

Nathan, Andrew (2003), 'Authoritarian Resilience', *Journal of Democracy*, vol. 14, no. 1, pp. 6–17.

Naughton, Barry (1995), *Growing out of the Plan: Chinese Economic Reform, 1978–1993*, New York: Cambridge University Press.

——— (2006) *The Chinese Economy: Transitions, and Growth*, Cambridge and London: MIT Press.

Ngai, Pun (1999), 'Becoming *Dagongmei* (Working Girls): The Politics of Identity and Difference in Reform China', *China Journal*, no. 42, pp. 1–18.

Offerlé, Michel (1993), *Un homme, une voix? Histoire du suffrage universel*, Paris: Gallimard.

Oi, Jean C. (1989), *State and Peasant in Contemporary China: The Political Economy of Village Government*, Berkeley: University of California Press.

——— (1999), *Rural China Takes Off: Institutional Foundations of Economic Reform*, Berkeley: University of California Press.

Oi, Jean C. and Zhao Shukai (2007), 'Direct Township Elections', in E. Perry and M. Goldman, *Grassroots Political Reform in Contemporary China*, Cambridge, MA: Harvard University Press.

O'Leary, Greg (ed.) (1997), *Adjusting to Capitalism: Chinese Workers and the State*, New York: M.E. Sharpe.

Palmer, David (2007), *Qigong Fever: Body, Science, and Utopia in China*, London: C. Hurst & Co.

Pasqualini, Jean [Bao, Ruowang] and Rudolph Chelminski (1975), *Prisoner of Mao*, London: André Deutsch.

Pearson, Margaret (1997), *China's New Business Elite: The Political Consequences of Reform*, Berkeley: University of California Press.

Peerenboom, Randall (2002), *China's Long March toward Rule of Law*, Cambridge: Cambridge University Press.

Pepper, Suzanne (1990), *China's Education Reform in the 1980s: Policies, Issues, and Historical Perspectives*, Berkeley: University of California Press.

Perry, Elizabeth and Mark Selden (eds) (2003), *Chinese Society: Change, Conflict and Resistance*, London and New York: Routledge.

Polanyi, Karl (1944), *The Great Transformation*, Boston: Beacon Press.

Pye, Lucian (1988), *The Mandarin and the Cadre*, Ann Arbor: Center for Chinese Studies.

Pringle, Tim (2011), *Trade Unions in China. The Challenge of Labour Unrest*, London and New York: Routledge.

Rocca, Jean-Louis (2006), *La Condition chinoise. La mise au travail capitaliste à l'âge des réformes (1978–2004)*, Paris: Karthala.

———— (ed.) (2008), *La Société chinoise vue par ses sociologues*, Paris: Presses de Sciences Po.

———— (2008), 'Power of Knowledge: The Imaginary Formation of the Chinese Middle Stratum in an Era of Growth and Stability', in Christophe Jaffrelot and Peter van der Veer (eds), *Patterns of Middle Class Consumption in India and China*, New Delhi: Sage.

———— (2013), 'Homeowners' Movements: Narratives on the Political Behaviours of the Middle Class' in David Goodman and Chen Minglu, *Middle Class China: Identity and Behaviour*, Edward Elgar, pp. 110–34.

Read, Benjamin (2012), *Roots of the State: Neighborhood Organizations and Social Networks in Beijing and Taipei*, Stanford, Stanford University Press.

Rofel, Lisa (2009), *Desiring China: Experiments in Neoliberalism, Sexuality, and Public Culture*, Durham, NC, and London: Duke University Press.

Shapiro, Judith (2012), *China's Environmental Challenges*, Cambridge, UK, and Maiden, MA: Polity Press.

Sheehan, Jackie (1998), *Chinese Workers: A New History*, London and New York: Routledge.

Shen, Jie (2007), *Labour Disputes and their Resolution in China*, Oxford: Chandos Publishing.

Shirk, Susan (1993), *The Political Logic of Economic Reform in China*, Berkeley: University of California Press.

Skocpol, Theda (ed.) (1984), *Vision and Method in Historical Sociology*, Cambridge: Cambridge University Press.

Smith, F. J. (2007), 'Chinese Oppression in Xinjiang, Middle Eastern conflicts and Global Islamic Solidarities among the Uighurs', *Journal of Contemporary China*, vol. 16, no. 53, November, pp. 627–54.

Song, Sophie (2014), 'Chinese College Graduates Cannot Secure Jobs: 28% Of Beijing's 2013 Graduates and 44% Of Shanghai's Have Found A Job', *International Business Times*, July 15 www.ibtimes.com/chinese-college-graduates-cannot-secure-jobs-28-beijings-2013-graduates-44-shanghais-have-found-job

Spence, Jonathan D. (1999), *The Search for Modern China*, New York: Norton.

Swedberg, Richard and Granovetter, Mark (eds) (1992), *The Sociology of Economic Life*, Boulder: Westview Press.

Thireau, Isabelle and Wang Hangsheng (eds) (2001), *Disputes au village chinois. Formes du juste et recompositions locales des espaces normatifs*, Paris: Éditions de la MSH.

Tang, Xiaojing (2009), *'Femmes au foyer', 'filles de fer' et retour au foyer. Genre et travail à Shanghai sur quatre générations, 1949–2007*, doctoral thesis in sociology, EHESS-ENS-ECNU.

Tong, Jingrong (2012), *Investigative Journalism in China: Journalism, Power, and Society*, New York and London: Continuum.

Walder, Andrew (1986), *Communist Neo-Traditionalism: Work and Authority in Chinese Industry*, Berkeley, Los Angeles and London: University of California Press.

Wank, David (1999), *Commodifying Communism: Business, Trust and Politics in a Chinese City*, Cambridge: Cambridge University Press.

Webber, Michael (2012), *Making Capitalism in Rural China*, Cheltenham, UK, and Northampton, MA: Edward Elgar.

Wedeman, Andrew (2012), *Double Paradox: Rapid Growth and Rising Corruption in China*, Ithaca, NY and London: Cornell University Press.

Whyte, Martin M., and William L. Parish (1978), *Village and Family in Contemporary China*, Chicago: University of Chicago Press.

—— (1984), *Urban Life in Contemporary China*, Chicago: University of Chicago Press.

Wu, Jane Jiajing (1991), 'Suicides and Suicide Survivors of the Cultural Revolution', in P. T. Bushnell et al (eds), *State Organized Terror: The Case of Violent Internal Repression*, Boulder: Westview Press, pp. 289–302.

Wu, Harry H. (1997), *Laogai, le goulag chinois*, Paris: Dagorno.

Yan, Yuxiang (2003), *Private Life under Socialism: Love, Intimacy, and Family Change in a Chinese Village, 1949–1999*, Stanford: Stanford University Press.

Yang, Mayfair (1994), *Gifts, Favors, and Banquets: The Art of Social Relationships in China*, Ithaca and London: Cornell University Press.

Yi, Lin (2008), *Cultural Exclusion in China: State Education, Social Mobility and Cultural Difference*, London and New York: Routledge.

Yu, Anthony C. (2004), *State and Religion in China*, Chicago and La Salle: Open Court.

Zhang, Kaining (ed.) (2012), *Sexual and reproductive Health in China: Reorienting Concepts and Methodology*, Leiden and Boston: Brill.

Zhang, Li (2010), *In Search of Paradise: Middle-Class Living in a Chinese Metropolis*, Ithaca, NY and London: Cornell University Press.

Zhang, Lian (2002), *The Tiananmen Papers*, London: Abacus.

Zhao, Dingxin (2001), *The Power of Tiananmen: state-society relations and the 1989 Beijing Student Movement*, Chicago: Chicago University Press.

Zhao, Weihua (2007), *Diwei yu xiaofei (Status and Consumption)*, Beijing: Shehui kexue wenxian chubanshe.

Zhou, Xiaohong, 'Chinese Middle Class: Reality or Illusion?' in Christophe Jaffrelot, and Peter Van der Veer (eds), *Patterns of Middle Class and Consumption in India and China*, New Delhi: Sage, pp. 110–26.

INDEX

169